LO ~~RABBIT~~

a guide to Cockney Rhyming Slang

by

Ian Wilkes

Illustrated by Ash

IAN HENRY PUBLICATIONS

Text © Ian Wilkes, 2004
Illustrations © Ashley Garrard, 2004

ISBN 0 86025 538 7

All characters in this book are fictitous
and any similarity to persons living or dead
is entirely coincidental

Published by
Ian Henry Publications, Ltd.
20 Park Drive, Romford, Essex RM1 4LH
and printed by
L.P.P.S.Ltd
128 Northampton Road, Wellingborough NN8 3PJ

INTRODUCTION

Over the years England's capital city has become home to many strangers, often speaking their own language – which was incomprehensible to the native Londoners. In self-defence some 150 years ago the Cockneys invented their own 'secret language', which is, in its turn, baffling to foreigners.

Cockney Rhyming Slang reached its full flowering at the turn of the 19th and 20th centuries, which is why there are so many references to music hall performers of that period and their songs.

However, it is a continually expanding language, always introducing new root words, although this can be self-defeating in that a secret language can only be comprehended if everyone is in on the joke.

Life can be made much more complicated to the unitiated listener when the second half of the rhyme is missing – and only the regular users know which phrases are treated thus.

This guide to Rhyming Slang has tried to ignore the Australian and American versions of the language and has not included terms that are likely to be ephemeral, generally when a film or pop star's name has had its fifteen minutes of fame and becomes yesterday's rhyme, to be superceded by a new catch phrase.

Therefore this book does not claim to be exhaustive, but the most common usages are represented.

The arrangement within this compilation is that the slang is given in **bold**, any explanation of the original follows in small type, the meaning(s) in plain type, explanations of the meanings are occasionally given, *and the sequence may end with the slang in a sentence in italic.*

The regular sequence is followed by a reverse dictionary of meanings, which shows that some objects have many versions in rhyming slang.

Acknowledgement must be given to the host of reference books consulted and to individuals who have contributed their examples, particularly Eddie Maguire, a real Mile End!

IHW

Linen draper

Abergavenny - Town in Gwent, South Wales - Penny

Adam and Eve - Original inhabitants of the Garden of Eden, see Genesis - Believe *"Would you Adam and Eve it!"*

Airs and graces - Braces / Faces / Races, especially Epsom *"Fred's off to the airs and graces Fursday."*

Alan Ladd - (1913-64) Hollywood star - Sad

Alan Whicker's - Television personality, born 1925 - Knickers

Alderman's eyes - Flies

Alive or dead - Head

All afloat - Boat

Alligator - Later *"See yer later, alligator." "In a while, crocodile."*

Almond rocks - Socks *"Please darn me almonds, Doris."*

Andy Pandy - Children's television puppet 1950-70s - Brandy

Anna Maria - [Domestic] Fire *"Shove some coal on the Anna before it goes out."*

Annie Laurie - (1682-1764) Of Maxwelton, Dumfries, married Alexander Ferguson. The verse was written by her rejected lover, William Douglas. It was set to music in 1835 by Lady John Scott - Lorry *"Fred's got a temp'ry job on the Annies."*

'A'penny dip - A small candle made by dipping a wick into melted tallow wax - Ship

Apple cider - Spider

Apple and banana - Joanna (Piano)

Apple fritter - Bitter beer

Apple pie - Sky

Apples and pears - Stairs

Apples and rice - Mice

April fool(s) - [Football] Pools *"Fred's won the April Fools."* / Tools / Stools

April showers - Flowers

Arf and arf - A half of mild and a half of bitter was a popular draught drink - Scarf

Aristotle - (384-322 B.C.) Greek philosopher, who wrote on most branches of learning including physics and biology - Bottle / Arse (see Bottle) *"Get your Aris off that cushion."*

Army and Navy - Gravy

Army tanks - Yanks

Artful Dodger - A youthful pickpocket in Charles Dickens' *Oliver Twist*. His given name was Jack Dawkins - Lodger - *"I hear that Marilyn's got a new artful."*

Arthur Rank - (1888-1972) business man, firstly in the flour trade, then in the cinema industry - Bank

Ash and oaks - Smokes

Aston Villa - Birmingham football team - Pillow

Aunt Ella - Umbrella

Auntie Cissie - Pissy *"Fred's had more than a couple and he's Auntie."*

Auntie Nellie - Belly

Autumn leaf - Thief

Ayrton Senna - Grand Prix racing driver - Tenner

Baa-lamb - Tram

Babbling brook - Cook *"The babbler baked a swan lake."* / Crook *"E's a tea leaf and a babbler to boot!"*

Back porch - Torch

Bacon rind - Blind

Baden Powells - Robert Baden-Powell (1857-1941), a military officer who founded the Boy Scouts (1907), Sea Scouts, Girl Guides, Wolf Cubs, and Rover Scouts - Bowels *"Fred's 'avin trouble with his Badens again."*

Bag of yeast - Priest

Baked beans – Haricot beans served in tomato sauce, usually tinned - Jeans *"Get yer backside into them baked beans."*

Baked potato - Waiter

Baker's dozen - Thirteen, from the 16th century custom of a baker adding an extra bun, which was the retailer's profit - Cousin

Ball of chalk - Walk

Ball of fat - Cat / Hat

Balloon car - Saloon Bar

Balmy breeze - Cheese

Band of Hope - A temperance organisation for young people founded in 1847 – Soap

Bangers and mash – Bangers is a slang expression for sausages - Cash

Barnaby Rudge - An historical novel by Charles Dickens, set at the time of the Gordon Riots in the 1780s – Judge

Barnet Fair - Dating back to 11th century, Barnet Fairs were a combination of horse, cattle, sheep and pleasure fairs, held at the beginning of September. There was also a horse race track, but this was abandoned when the railway was built in 1871. By 1876 the comment was made, 'The pleasure fair continued, but it has become such a scene of ruffianism that its early suppression may be anticipated.'- Hair *"Your Barnet could do with an Old Folks."*

Barney Rubble - a character in the cartoon *The Flintstones* - Trouble *"Steer clear of him, he's nothin' but Barney."*

Bat and wicket - Ticket

Bath bun - Son / Sun

Battle cruiser - A warship with less heavy armour than a battleship, but with the speed of a cruiser - Boozer *"See yer down the Battle later?"*

Bear's paw - Saw

Beecham's Pills - A patent medicine invented and marketed by Thomas Beecham (1820-1907) -'Worth a guinea a box.' - Bills *"Fred's up before the Beak for not paying his Beecham's."*

Beecher's Brook - A water hazard on the Aintree race course - Cook / Look

Beef and mutton - Glutton

Beehive - Dive *"The ref said Alf didn't trip 'im, but Fred took a beehive deliberate."*

Bees and honey - Money

Beg your pardon - Garden

Beggar boy's ass - Brass (money)

Beggar-my-Neighbour - a card game for two players where the object is to win all one's opponent's cards. It dates back over two hundred years - Labour [exchange]

Belt and braces - Horse race meetings

Ben Hur - A novel, by Lew Wallace (1880), set in ancient Rome; its film is remembered as featuring a chariot race - Stir (prison)

Bended knees - Cheese

Benny Hill - (1925-92) Comedian - Till (cash register)

Bernard Dillon - Villain

Bernhard Langer - Golfer - Banger (sausage)

Bicycle spanner - Tanner - A tanner was sixpence in real money – now worth two and a half pence

Billy Bunter - The fat comic character 'The Owl of the Remove' created by Frank Richards (1876-1961) - Punter

Birch broom - Room

Bird lime - Time in prison *"Mick's doing bird for nicking an Annie."*

Biscuits and cheese - Knees

Blackadder - A comedy character portrayed by Rowan Atkinson in the television series - Ladder

Black Maria - The police van for the conveyance of prisoners, named after Maria Lee, a burly Negress who helped Boston Police carry offenders - Fire (emergency and not a domestic fire)

Blackbird and thrush - Brush

Blackwall Tunnel - A Thames tunnel connecting Poplar and North Greenwich, built in 1897 - Ship's funnel

Bladder of lard - Card / Scotland Yard - Great Scotland Yard, Whitehall, was the headquarters of the Metropolitan Police 1842-91; New Scotland Yard, Parliament Street, was then used until 1967, when 'Scotland Yard' was transferred to Broadway, Victoria Street. In the Middle Ages, Scotland Yard was the London residence of the kings of Scotland.

Block and tackle - Shackle (hand-cuffs)

Block of ice - Dice

Blue moon - First mentioned in 16th century to mean 'very rare' - Spoon

Bo Peep - Little Miss Peep was careless with her flock. Nursery rhyme - Sleep

Boat Race - Contest started in 1829 between Oxford and Cambridge University crews: now on the River Thames between Putney and Mortlake - Face

Bob Hope - (1903-2003) American comedian born in Eltham, London - Dope

Bob Squash - Wash

Bobbie Moore - (1941-93) footballer - Door

Boiled rag - Hag

Bonnie Dundee - John Graham of Claverhouse, first Viscount Dundee (1649?-89). Scottish military hero - Flea

Boracic lint - A simple dressing for small cuts and grazes - Skint *"Sorry I can't help, I'm brassic - as usual."*

Borrow and beg - Egg

Bottle and glass - Arse

Bottle and stopper - Copper

Bottle of sauce - Horse

Bottle of water - Daughter

Bow and arrow - Sparrow

Bowler hat - A stiff felt hat with a round crown and narrow brim, invented by John Bowler, 19th century hatmaker - Rat

Box of toys - Noise

Box of tricks - Flicks - Cinema, taken from the time when cinemas showed silent, flickery, films - *"I'm going to the Box to see Lord of the Rings."*

Brace and bits - Tits

Brahms and Liszt - Johannes Brahms (1833-97) and Franz Liszt (1811-86), composers. - Pissed *"Fred's more Brahms than usual tonight, ducky."*

Brass nail - Tail [prostitute] *"If he goes with that tail again, I'll kill 'im, then divorce 'im."*

Brass tacks - Facts

Bread and butter - Gutter / Nutter *"Fred broke into the police station? I always did say he was a bread."*

Bread and cheese - Knees / Sneeze

Bread and honey - Money

Bread and jam - Tram *"Fred's bin sacked again; he tried to get his tram past the one in front."*

Brewer's bung - Tongue

Brian O'Lynn - Gin

Bricks and mortar - Daughter

Bride and groom - Broom

Bright and frisky - Whisky

Brighton Pier - There have been three piers in Brighton, but that referred to here is almost certainly the Palace Pier, opened in 1899 - Queer *"He's as Brighton as they come."*

Brighton Rock - Graham Greene's screened novel (1947) - Courtroom dock

Bristol City - Football club - Titty *"She has the most fantastic Bristols in the Borough."*

Brother and sister - Blister

Brother and sisters - Whiskers

Brown bread - Dead *"Cripes, he's brown Bread."*

Brussels sprout - Boy Scout / Tout (sells tickets at high prices)

Bryant and Mays - Match manufacturers; notorious for their workers contracting phossy jaw - gangrene caused by phosphorus poisoning - Stays - Metal or whalebone supports in corsetry

Bubble and squeak - Cold boiled potato and cooked cabbage fried together. They first bubbled in boiling water, then squeaked in the frying pan. - Beak *"'E's comin' up in front of the squeak."* / Greek *"Although he's only a waiter, he's very nice for a Bubble."* / Weak (sick) / Week (7 days is a bubble)

Buccaneer - Queer

Buck and doe - Snow

Bucket and pail - Jail *"That tea leaf's off to the bucket."*

Buckle Me Shoe - One two, buckle my shoe, a children's counting rhyme - Jew *"Very generous, that buckleme."*

Bull and cow - Row *"Bill and Marge had a right Bull and Cow."*

Bullock's horn - Pawn

Bully beef - Tinned corned beef used as military rations – Chief Officer (in prison)

Bunsen Burner - Laboratory instrument named after Robert Wilhelm Bunsen - Earner *"That bank job was a nice little bunsen."*

Burnt cinder - Window

Burton on Trent - Staffordshire town, mainly known in London as a centre of brewing - Rent

Bushel and peck - Units of volume, four pecks to one bushel, which is equal to 2,219 cubic inches - Cheque / Neck

Bushey Park - The south entrance to Bushey Park is opposite the Lion Gate of Hampton Court Gardens. The famous avenue of horse chestnuts was planted by William III. Public access was secured in 1752 by Timothy Bennet, shoe-maker of Hampton Wick - Lark *"He was jumping around, having a right Bushey."*

Butcher's hook - Look *"'Ere, come and have a butcher's at this."*

Cabman's Rest - In Victorian London there were established a number of good-pull-ins for cabbies in various squares. A few still exist, e.g. Temple Place - Breast

Cain and Able - The children of Adam and Eve, whose story is told in *Genesis* - Table

Camden Town - A district in north-west London, known for its Market. Its station was opened in 1850 - Brown

Canal boat - Tote

Canoe(s) - Shoes

Cape Horn - The most southerly point of South America in Chile - Dawn

Cape of Good Hope - A promentory at the southern end of Africa (not, however, the most southerly point) - Soap

Captain Bligh - William Bligh (1754-1817) was in the mutiny on the *Bounty* in 1789. Later Governor of New South Wales - Pie

Captain Cook - James Cook (1728-79) circumnavigator: mapped much of the Pacific Ocean - Book

Captain Merry - Sherry

Carl Rosa - From the opera company founded in 1875 - Poser
"Don't trust that Wayne, he's a right Carl Rosa."

Carlo Gatti - Company that supplied ice cream to London restaurants - Batty

Carving knife - Wife

Casey's Court – A children's strip cartoon first appearing in *Illustrated Chips* in 1902 - Port

Cash and carry - Marry

Cat and kitties - Titties

Cat and mouse - House

Cat's milk - Silk

Cats and mice - Dice

Cellar flap - Tap *"He's marvellous with his dancing, 'specially his Cellar."* / Tap *"She's never bin any good with her money. So she's always on the Cellar."*

Chalfont St Giles - The Buckinghamshire village to which John Milton retired in his blindness. Nearby is Jordans, where William Penn, the founder of Pennsylvania, is buried in the graveyard of the Society of Friends meeting place – Piles *"Fred's got a dose of the Chalfonts."*

Chalk Farm(s) - A district in north-west London between Camden and Belsize Park - Arm(s) / Harm

Charing Cross - The site of the hamlet of Charing in the time of Edward I, who set up there one of the Eleanor Crosses in memory of his wife. It became a terminal for the South Eastern and Chatham Railway in 1859 - Horse

Charley Freer - Beer

Charley Howard - Coward

Charley Prescott - Waistcoat

Charlie Dilke - Sir Charles Wentworth Dilke (1843-1911), tipped as a future Prime Minister, but got involved in a divorce suit in 1885 - Milk

Charlie Drake - Comedian born 1925 - Brake

Charlie Mason - Basin *"I'll 'ave a Charlie Masonfull of that puddin', please."*

Chas and Dave - Music hall pianists of the 1980s - Shave

Cheerful giver - Liver

Cheese and kisses - Missus

Cheese grater - Waiter

Chelsea bun - A rolled currant bun - Son

Cherry hog - Dog, especially a greyhound *"I'm going to the Cherries at Romford this evening."*

Cherry ripe - An old street call by itinerant vendors - Pipe *"He asked that his favourite Cherry be buried with him."* / Tripe *"I've never heard such a load of old Cherry."*

Chevy Chase - The Percy family of Northumberland illegally hunted in the Scottish border country; this was recalled in a ballad of the same name - Face *"I'd remember his Chevy anywhere."*

Chicken and rice - Nice

China plate - Mate *"Fred's bin a china of mine since we was kids together."*

Christmas cards - The custom of sending Christmas cards began in England in the 1860s - Guards - lookout, railway guard / Grenadier Guard

Christmas crackered - Knackered

Christmas Eve - 24th December, the feast of St Stephen - Believe

Cigarette holder - Shoulder

Clever Mike - Bike

Clodhopper - A country bumpkin - Copper

Clothes pegs - Legs

Coachman on the box - Pox *"Fred's got the coachman's – again."*

Coal and coke - Broke

Cobblers' awls - Small tool used for pricking leather - Balls *"What a load of cobblers!"*

Cock and hen - Ten pound note

Cock linnet - "I followed on with me old cock linnet." Part of *My old man said 'Follow the van, Don't dilly-dally on the way'*, music hall song, popularised by Marie Lloyd (1870-1922) - Minute *"Hang on a tick, I won't be 'arf a cock linnet."*

Cock sparrow - Barrow - especially for market traders

Cockroach - Motor Coach *"We're goin' on a cockroach all the way to the Costa Packet!"*

Cold potato - Waiter *"I wish that cold potater'd 'urry up!"*

Collar and cuff - Pouffe

Collar and tie - Lie

Colney Hatch - The Middlesex Lunatic Asylum was founded near Friern Barnet in 1851. By 1877 there were about 800 men and 1,200 women superintended by 300 officers - Match *"You goin' to Arsenal's Colney with Spurs?"*

Come a clover - Trip over

Conan Doyle - Sir Arthur Conan Doyle (1859-1930), novelist and psychic researcher, renowned as creator of Sherlock Holmes, Doctor Watson and Professor Moriarty - Boil *"Fred's got a fearful Conan on his fife."*

Copper's nark - Car park

Corn flake - A breakfast cereal made from toasted maize - Fake

Corns and bunions - Onions, but also implies knowledge. *"She knows 'er corns an' bunions."*

Cough and choke - Smoke

Cough and sneeze - Cheese

Cough and splutter - Butter

Council houses - Trousers

Country cousin - Dozen, used mainly on the race course

Cousin Ella - Umbrella

Cousin Nellie - Belly

Covent Garden - Originally the burial ground of the Convent of Westminster. In the 17th century the fruit, flower and vegetable market started, with permanent buildings in 1850. The market moved to Nine Elms in 1974 - Pardon *"The Appeal Judge give 'im a Covent Garden."*

Cow and calf - Laugh

Cow's lick - The Nick

Cream crackered - Nackered *"Blimey, Fred, after that run, I'm cream crackered!"*

Crust of bread - Head *"Ouch! Right on the crust!"* / Lead

Cuddle and kiss - Miss *"She's a right stuck up Cuddle."*

Currant bread - Dead

Currant bun - Run *"Roger's got out of Maidstone and he's on the Currant."* / Son / Sun - the planet, but also the newspaper

Custard and jelly - Telly

Cut and carried - Married

Cuts and scratches - Matches

Daffadown Dilly - Silly *"That is an absolutely daffy idea!"*

Daft and barmy - The army

Daily Mail - Newspaper founded on 4th May, 1896 - Ale

Daisy roots - Boots

Dan Dares - The *Eagle* comic hero - Flares (trousers)

Danny la Rue - Female impersonator, real name Daniel Carroll (born 1927) - Clue *"That copper hasn't got a Danny about the break-in."*

Darby and Joan - Old-fashioned, virtuous, old couple in a ballad written by Henry Woodfall in 1735. The originals are said to be John Darby and his wife - Alone *"Now she's a widder she spends too much time on her Darby."*

Davy Crocket - (1786-1836) American frontiersman: a member of the House of Representatives for Tennessee, he died defending the Republic of Texas at the Battle of Alamo — Pocket *"You put your hand in yer Davy this time, Fred."*

Day and night - Light ale

Day's a-dawning - Morning

Dead beat - Meat

Deep sea diver - Fiver

Deep South - The southernmost states of the U. S. A. - Mouth

Derby brights - Coal - Lights

Derby Kelly - "That's the stuff for yer Derby Kell, it makes yer fit and it keeps yer well." Part of the refrain of *Boiled Beef and Carrots*, music hall song popularised by Harry Champion - Belly

Derry and Toms - Department store in Kensington - Bombs *"Kevin says there was more Derries flying around in the Blitz than you can believe."*

Dickory dock - 'Hickory dickory dock, the mouse ran up the clock...' Nursery rhyme - Clock *"Is that dickory right?"*

Dicky bird - Word *"I'd like a dicky bird in yer King Lear."*

Dicky Dirt – Shirt *"'e looks smart in that frilled dicky, don't 'e?"*

Dig in the grave - Shave *"I'll be with you when I've got me dicky on an' had a dig."*

Ding dong - Sing Song

Ding Dong Bell - 'Ding, dong, bell, pussy's in the well...' Nursery rhyme - Hell

Doctor Crippen - Hawley Harvey Crippen (1862-1910), poisoner of his wife. The first man arrested as a result of trans-Atlantic wireless telegraphy - Dripping

Dog and bone - Telephone

Dog and cat - Mat

Doggett's Coat and Badge – Orange livery with a silver badge competed for by Thames watermen since 1715, making it the oldest sculling race in the world. Thomas Doggett (d.1721) was an Irish comic actor. - Cadge *"You're on the Doggett's again!"*

Dolly mixtures - Pictures *"Jim's taking me to the dollies tonight."*

Dolly Varden - In Charles Dickens' *Barnaby Rudge*, a character who wore a large hat trimmed with flowers - Garden

Door knob - Bob - The colloquial term for a shilling in real money – five pence today

Dot and carried - To dot and carry is to limp - Married

Dover Harbour - Used since pre-Roman times as the principal port of entry to England from continental Europe - Barber

Down the drains - Brains

Doyly Carte - Richard D'Oyly Carte (1844-1901), producer of most of the Gilbert and Sullivan operas at the Savoy Theatre - Fart *"If ye're goin' to Doyly again, go outside fer Gawd's sake."*

Dripping toast - Host   *"The dripping at the Crown's thrown Fred out."*

Drum and fife - Knife / Wife

Duchess of Fife - Louise Victoria Alexandra Dagmar (1867-1931) Princess Royal, third child of Prince of Wales, married Duke of Fife in 1889 - Wife

Duchess of Teck - Parent of Queen Mary, consort of George V - Cheque

Duchess of York - Sarah Ferguson became Duchess of York on marrying Elizabeth II's third son - Pork

Duck and dive - Hide / Skive / Survive

Duke of Kent - A royal dukedom, the Duke probably remembered here is George Edward Alexander Edmund (1902-42), fourth son of George V - Bent, mishapen or dishonest (a bent copper) / Rent

Duke of York - 'The Grand Old Duke of York' was Frederick Augustus, duke of York and Albany (1763-1827), second son of George III, commanded English army in Flanders, 1793-5, commander in chief, 1798-1809 - Cork (in a bottle) / Fork as used for eating / Talk

Dull and dowdy - Cloudy (weather)

Dunkirk - Evacuation beaches of the British Expeditionary Force May-June, 1940, by the Little Ships and the Royal Navy - Work

Dunlop tyre - John Boyd Dunlop (1840-1921) was the inventor of the pneumatic rubber tyre - Liar

Dustbin lid - Kid

Dutch - "We've bin together nah for forty years and it don't seem a day too much, there ain't a lidy livin' in the land as I'd swop for me dear old Dutch." Sentimental ballad by Albert Chevalier (1861-1923) *see* Duchess of Fife

Dutch pegs - Legs

Early bird - Word

Early door - Whore

Early doors - Some music halls let the cheaper seats get settled before the better-off patrons were let in - Drawers

Early hour(s) - Flower(s) especially by sellers in the market

Earwig - Twig   *"Do I earwig you correct, squire?"*

East and West - Chest / Vest

Easter bunny - Money

Easter egg - The custom of making gifts of eggs to children at Easter probably derives from paschal payments from villeins to their overlord - Leg

Eau de Cologne - A perfumed spirit invented by Johann Maria Farina in 1799. Twelve drops each of bergamot, citron, neroli, orange, rosemary and a gallon of rectified spirit - 'Phone

Edmundo Ros - Latin American band leader, born 1910 - Boss

Edward Heath - Sir Edward Heath (born 1916), a Member of Parliament from 1950 to 1997. Conservative Prime Minister from 1970-74 - Teeth

Eiffel Tower - An iron tower on the left bank of the Seine in Paris, 984 feet tall, designed by A G Eiffel (1832-1923) for the Paris Exhibition of 1889 – Shower of rain

Eighteen pence - One shilling and sixpence in pre-decimal money, now worth seven and a half pence - Fence *"Fred only got a thankyou from his eighteen pence for that tiarra."* / Sense *"Where's yer eighteen pence gorn?"*

Elastic bands - Hands

Elephant's trunk - Drunk

Engineers and stokers - Brokers *"Fred's had the engineers round and they took back his Marie Corelli."*

English Channel - The body of water between England and France extending 350 miles from the Strait of Dover to a line from the Isles of Scilly to Ushant. It varies in width from 21 to 350 miles - Panel [National Health Service] *"Fred's on the English again."*

Epsom Races - Dating back to James I, but established formally about 1730. The Derby was started by Edward, 12th Earl of Derby in 1780; the Oaks (after his house of that name in nearby Woodmansterne) by the same gentleman in 1779. Epsom Downs, particularly Derby Day, have been a highlight in the racing calendar since the start of the railways - Braces

Ernie Marsh - Grass

Errol Flynn - (1909-59) Australian-born Hollywood film star, remembered for his swashbuckling rôles as Captain Blood and Robin Hood - Chin *"Go on, Sid. Give 'im one on the Errol."*

Everton toffee - A district of Liverpool, renowned for its sweets factory and football team - Coffee

Eyes of blue - True *"Wot I'm tellin' you is a hundred per cent eyes of blue."*

False alarms - Arms

Far and near - Beer

Farmer Giles - Piles *"Look at Fred shufflin', he's got a dose of the farmer's."*

Feather and flip - Kip *"I'm off for a feather."*

Fellow-feeling - Ceiling

Field of wheat - Street *"If only the sweepers'd come down 'ere once in a while it'd be a nice field of wheat."*

Fife and drum - Bum

Fillet of plaice - Face *"Wash yer fillet wiv band of 'ope."*
Fine and dandy - Brandy
Finger and thumb - Drum [a traveller's word for road] / Mum / Rum
Fireman's hose - Nose *"Stop pickin' yer fireman's, Wayne."*
Fisherman's daughter - Water
Flag unfurled - World
Flea and louse - House with a bad reputation
Fleas and ants - Pants
Flounder and dab - Cab *"Bill's passed the Knowledge and now he's got a flounder of his own."*
Flowers and frolics - Bollocks
Flowery dell - Cell *"I've bin in this flowery dell for too long."*
Fly by nights - Tights *"Hang on a minute, I'm just getting me fly bys on."*

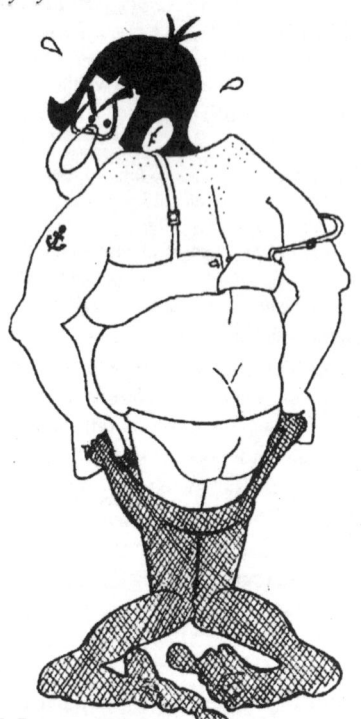

Fly tipper - Nipper (child)
Flying trapeze - 'He'd fly through the air with the greatest of ease, a daring young man on the flying trapeze' music hall song (1868) by George Leybourne - Cheese

Forbidden fruit - Loot

Fork and knife - Life / Wife

Fortnum and Mason – Up-market grocers in Piccadilly founded in 1707 by William Fortnum and Hugh Mason - Basin

Four by two - Jew *"That Hymie is the nicest Four-be in 'ackney."*

Fourpenny bit - A small silver coin of the 18th century – Hit *"Fred gave him a fourpenny one, right on his lug."*

Fourth of July - Independence Day in America - Tie

Fox and hound - Round of drinks. *"Whose fox an' 'ound is it?"*

France and Spain - Rain

Frank and Hank - Bank

Frock and frill - Chill *"Fred's gone down with a frock."*

Frog and toad - Road

Front wheel skid - Yid

Funny face(s) - Lace(s) for shoes or boots

Gamble and Proctor - Multinational food manufacturers - Doctor

Game of Nap - Card game, named after Napoleon III. The maximum number of tricks that can be made is five - Cap

Gammon rasher - Smasher *"That Judy's a right gammon."*

Garden gate - Magistrate *"Fred's up before the gardens again."*

Garden gates - Rates and taxes

Garden gnome - Comb

Gay and frisky - Whisky

Gay Gordon - A traditional Scottish dance; also the Gordon Highlanders - Traffic warden

Gazunder - The popular name for chamber pot, because it gazunder the bed - Punter

General Booth - (1829-1912) William Booth, founder of the Salvation Army - Tooth

George Raft - (1895-1980) Hollywood heavy - Draught *"There's a terrible George Raft in here."* / Graft

German band(s) - Itinerant German brass bands were popular at the turn of the 19th/20th century. In the music hall song *Down at the Old Bull and Bush* it says "hear the little German band, tar-ra-ra-ra-ra-ra..." - Hand(s) *"Look at the state of your Germans!"*

Gert and Daisy - Elsie and Doris Waters' double act on the music halls and radio - Lazy *"Anyone else'd have put that shelf up by now, but you're so Gert and Daisy!"*

Gertie Gitana - (1888-1957) 'A sort of music hall legend' [*Your own, your very own!* by Peter Gammond] - Banana

Ginger ale - Jail

Ginger beer - Queer *"He's as ginger as nine bob note."*

Gingerbread - Head

Girls and boys - Noise

Give and take - Cake

Glasgow Rangers - Scottish football club - Strangers *"Look out, Fred, there's some Glasgows comin'."*

Glass case - Face

Glass of beer - Ear

Glass of plonk - Conk, nose

God almighty - 'Praise to the Lord! the Almighty, the King of Creation!' 1863 hymn translated by Catherine Winkworth (1827-78) from the German of Joachim Neander (1650-80) - Nightdress

God forbid - 'And when they heard it, they said, God forbid'. Bible, St Luke, ch20,v16 - Lid [hat] / Yid

God forbids - Kids *"That Marilyn's got more godfers than you can count!"*

God save the Queens - 'God save our gracious King! Long live our noble King!' attributed to various authors, including Henry Carey (c1687-1743) – Greens

Gold watch - Scotch *"I fancy a spot of gold watch."*

Golden Hind - Ship in which Francis Drake circumnavigated the world 1577-80 - Blind

Golliwogs - Black dolls designed by Florence Upton (1873-1922) to illustrate her sister's stories. Adopted as a mascot by Robinson's marmalade manufacturers - The dogs *"I'm off to the gollies."*

Goodie and baddie - Paddy (an Irishman)

Goose's neck - Cheque *"I've got no ready, but I'll give you a gooses for the custard."*

Gooseberry pudden - The old woman [wife]

Gordon and Gotch - Book and magazine importers - Watch

Gospel Oak - Suburb between Kentish Town and Hampstead - Joke

Grasshopper - Copper [policeman] / Informer [shopper]

Greengage - Stage *"Our Rita's goin' on the greengage."*

Greengages - Wages *"Fred's getting regular greens at last!"*

Gregory Peck - Hollywood actor, born 1916 - Neck *"Get that down your Gregory!"*

Grey mare - 'Tom Pearse, Tom Pearse, lend me your grey mare' the first line of the ballad *Widdecombe Fair* - Bus fare

Grimsby Docks - Lincolnshire fishing port – Socks

Groucho Marx - (1890-1977) The leader of the film/vaudeville Marx Brothers - Sparks (electrician)

Grumble and mutter - Flutter *"Fred's done a grumble on the Airs."*

Guinea pig - Wig

Gunga Din - 'Though I've belted you and flayed you, By the livin' Gawd that made you, You're a better man than I am, Gunga Din!' Verse by Rudyard Kipling (1865-1936) - Chin

Guy Fawkes – (1570-1606) Gunpowder plotter - Walks

Gypsy's kiss - Piss *"Where's yer bog? I'm dyin' for a gypsies."*

Gypsy's warning - Morning

Hackney Marsh(es) - An area of east London that is taken up with a large range of sporting activities - Glass(es) for drinking / Spectacles *"I left me 'ackneys on the mantlepiece 'smorning."*

Hail and rain - Train

Hairy goat - Throat

Hale and hearty - A party

Half a dollar - Coined when there were roughly four American dollars to a pound sterling - therefore two shillings and sixpence - Collar

Half hitch - A knot made by looping a rope around an object and then back around itself, bringing the rope through the loop - Snitch *"That bloke half-hitched that old geezer's wallet."*

Half inch - Pinch *"Fred half-inched that telly over there."*

Half ouncer - Bouncer *"Fred's standin' in for the half ouncer down at the bingo."*

Half past two - Jew

Halfpenny dip - *see* 'A'penny dip

Halfpenny stamp - Tramp

Ham and bone - Home

Ham shank - Yank

Hampstead Heath - Until 1700 the Middlesex elections were held on the Heath. Then its 240 acres became a pleasure ground, attracting 50,000 people for the Whit-Monday holiday. Renowned for views to the Surrey, Hampshire and Essex hills. Two pubs, the Bull and Bush and Jack Straw's Castle, have historic connections – Teeth *"He give 'im such a slosh in the Hampsteads."*

Hand and fist - Pissed

Handley Page - Sir Frederick Handley Page (1885-1962) aircraft designer and manufacturer. Produced mainly bombing aircraft for the Great War and transport planes for WWII and after - The Stage

Hansel and Gretel - Abandoned waifs in the Grimm fairy tale - Kettle

Hansom cab - A low-hung two-wheeled cabriolet holding two persons inside, the driver being mounted on a dickey behind and the reins going over the roof. Invented by Joseph Alyosius Hansom (1803-82) in 1834 - Scab (a strike breaker)

Harbour light - Right *"It's all harbour."*

Hard labour - Neighbour

Harry Lauder - (1870-1950) Scottish comedian and composer, knighted in 1919 - Order

Harry Nash - Cash

Harry Randall - (1860-1932) Patter comedian on the music halls - Candle / Handle

Harry Tate - (1873-1940) Comedian, noted for his motoring and fishing sketches, remembered for his outrageous false moustaches - Late / State *"I'm in a right old Harry Tate."*

Harry Wragg - Jockey and trainer - Fag *"I've run out, so give us a Harry, would yer?"*

Harvey Nichols - Upper crust shop established in 1813 by Benjamin Harvey on the corner of Sloane Street and Knightsbridge - Pickles

Has beens - Greens (vegetables)

Hat and coat - Refrigerated boat

Hat and feather - Weather

Hat and scarf - Bath

Hearth rugs - Bedbugs / Mugs

Hearts of Oak - 'Heart of oak are our ships, Heart of oak are our men...' Song by David Garrick (1717-79) - Broke *"I'd help if I could, but I'm hearts 'til Friday."*

Heaven and hell - Smell

Heavens above - Love

Hedge and ditch - Pitch [playing area] / Market pitch

Helter skelter - Tower at a fun fair with a spiral track down which one slides on a mat - Shelter *"The Helter ain't much, but it's better than dossing in the field of wheat."*

Henley Regatta - Water-based event in the social calendar - Natter *"Why don't you pop in for a Henley on Tuesday?"*

Here and there - Chair *"Pull up an 'ere an' there and I'll tell you all about it."*

Herring and kipper - Stripper

Hi Diddle Diddle - 'Hi diddle diddle, the cat and the fiddle, the cat ran away with the spoon...' Nonsense nursery rhyme - Fiddle *"He's on the hi diddle diddle."*

Hi Jimmy Knacker - Victorian street game - Tobacco

Hide and seek - Cheek

High stepper - Pepper

Highland fling - Sing

Hill and dale - Tale *"Fred'll spin you a hill and dale that'll bring tears to your minces."*

Hit and miss - Piss

Hit or miss - Kiss

Hobbledehoy - Boy, especially a troublesome adolescent

Hobson's Choice - Thomas Hobson (1544?-1631), a Cambridge carrier, who always refused to let any of his horses out of its proper turn - Voice *"You've got a beautiful 'obson's, Marleen."*

Hokey-pokey - Italian ice cream - Chokey (prison)

Holy friar - Liar *"He's pullin' yer leg, he's a right Holy friar."*

Holy Ghost - The third person of the Christian Trinity - Post (on the race course). *"The 'orses are at the 'oly."* / Toast *"Could you butter me a slice of 'oly, please."*

Holy water - Daughter

Home on the range - 'Home, home on the range, where the deer and the buffalo play'. Western American ditty - Strange

Hong Kong - British colony 1842-1997 on the Chinese coast - Pong *"You don't half Hong Kong, Fred - where've you bin?"* / Wrong

Horse and carriage - Garage

Horse and trough - Cough *"You 'ave got a nasty 'orse."*

Horses and carts - Darts

Hot Cross Bun - A sweet bun with raisins and with a cross of pastry on top; traditionally eaten on Good Friday - Gun / Run *"Fred's on the 'ot cross from the p'lice."* / Son

Hot potato - Waiter

Hounslow Heath - West London area renowned for highwaymen and gibbets - Teeth

House of Lords - Corduroy trousers

House to let - Bet

Housemaid's knee – A chronic, inflammatory swelling of the back of the knee, caused by prolonged kneeling on hard floors - The sea

Housey-housey - Game now known as bingo - Lousy

How D'ye Do - 'Here's a how-de-do! If I marry you..." lyric from *The Mikado* (1885) by W S Gilbert - Stew *"She'd lost 'er bat an' wicket an' was in a proper 'ow d'ye do."*

Hugs and kisses - Missus

Hurricane lamp - Tramp

I suppose - Nose

Ice-cream freezer - Geezer, any adult

Ideal Home - The exhibition runs at Earls Court in the spring - Comb

In and Out - Nickname of the Naval & Military Club, 94 Piccadilly - Stout

Inky blue - Influenza

Inky smudge - Judge

Irish jig - Wig *"Is that a new Irish wot Fred's wearin'?"*

Irish Rose - Nose

Irish stew - True *"That's too bloody Irish for words!"*

Iron Duke - Nickname of the Duke of Wellington (Arthur Wellesley) (1769-1852), victor of Waterloo and, later, Prime Minister - Fluke

Iron girder - Murder *"Wayne can get away with iron girder with his dad."*

Iron horse - Race course

Iron tank - Bank

Isle of Man - Island in the Irish Sea, an autonomous possession of the British Crown. Its Tynwald (Parliament) is over a thousand years old - Fan *"That Melvyn is a right Isle of Man of yours, Cynthia."*

Isle of Wight - An island off the south coast, separated from the mainland by the Solent and Spithead channels. Popular holiday place, known to the Romans as Vectis - Right, as in direction and correctness / Tight, as in keeping hold of one's money / Tight, as in drunk

Itch and scratch - Match *"Got any itches on you?"*

Jack a Dandy - Brandy

Jack and Jill - Originate in the Scandinavian deities Hjuki and Bil, captured by the moon god Mani as they went to draw water, and still visible along with their pail in the moon's markings - Bill, demands for money / Hill / Pill used by drug users / Till or cash register

Jack Frost - The personification of frosty weather first recorded early 19th century - Lost

Jack Jones - Alone *"You're on yer Jack when you're divorced."*

Jack Ketch - (d.1686) The common executioner from 1663 of, among others, the Duke of Monmouth - Stretch (in prison)

Jack Tar - Nickname for a sailor, first recorded in the 18th century - Bar, especially riverside or harbour bar

Jack Randall - A bare-knuckle pugilist mid-19th century - Candle

Jack Sprat - Nursery rhyme character who, with his wife, cleaned his plate - Meat fat / Brat

Jack the Ripper - A series of murders of prostitutes in Whitechapel in 1888 was claimed by 'Jack the Ripper' - never positively identified - Kipper / Slipper

Jacket and vest - West [End of London] *"I'm goin' up the jacket termorrer."*

Jam jar - Car *"I wouldn't mind so much, but 'e wrapped the jam round the lamppost, so we can't go out and we can't see outside neither."*

Jam roll - Dole / Parole

Jam tart - Sweetheart

Jamaica Rum - A spirit distilled from molasses derived from sugar cane - Thumb

Jekyll and Hyde - A Gothic novel (1886) by Robert Louis Stevenson - Snide (counterfeit)

Jenny Lee - Labour politician, married to Aneurin Bevan. Member of Parliament 1929-31, 1945-70. Education Minister in the Wilson government - Tea

Jenny Lind - (1820-87) Swedish soprano - Wind *"Fred's got a touch of the Jenny Lind today."*

Jeremiah - A prophet of the seventh and sixth centuries B.C. - Fire, domestic

Jerusalem artichoke - The tuber of the Jerusalem artichoke, a North American sunflower, eaten as a vegetable - Moke [Donkey] - *The Jeerusalem's dead* was a music hall song performed by Albert Chevalier.

Jew chum - Bum (tramp)

Jim Prescott - Waistcoat

Jim Skinner - Dinner

Jimmy O'Goblin - Sovereign - The gold pound that was withdrawn from circulation in 1917

Jimmy Riddle - Piddle (*cf* Riddle me ree)

Joan of Arc - (c1412-31) French national heroine - Park

Joanna - Piano *"Fred can play a jo like that Liberace."*

Joe Blake – (1688-1724) Pickpocket, cut-throat and robber. Hung - Stake or bet

Joe Brown - Town

Joe Gurr - Stir (prison)

Joe Hook - Crook

Joe Savage - Cabbage

Joe Soap - A dope *"Fred's missing a ha'penny in the shilling – he's a right Joe Soap."*

John O'Groat - Popularly (but not accurately) the northern extremity of mainland Scotland, named after John de Groat, a Dutchman who built an octagonal house there in the 16th century - Coat

John Wayne - (1907-79) American film star. Real name Marion Michael Morrison - Train

Johnny Cash - (1932-2003) Country music singer - Slash *"Fred's gone to have a Johnny round the back of the bus shelter."*

Johnny Horner - Nursery rhyme about a boy in a corner can be traced to 1720; said to relate to the abbot of Glastonbury's steward who, at the dissolution of the monasteries in 1558, acquired the deeds of the manor of Mells by a trick - Corner *"Fred's gone round the Johnny 'orner and'll be back in a tick."*

Joint of beef - Chief or boss

Jolly Roger - The pirate flag, derived from the Tamil *Ali Raja* - Lodger

Jonah's whale - Old Testament episode - Tail

Judy and Punch - Puppet show drama brought to England from Italy at the end of the 17th century. Punch is dissipated, violent and cunning: consequently popular - Lunch

Julius Caesar - (100-44 BC) Roman general and dictator - Freezer

Kangaroo - An Australian marsupial, possibly so called when an Aboriginal was asked 'What is that animal's name?' and replied that he did not know - Jew *"Mannie's the only kanga living in this street."* / Screw (prison warder)

Kate Carney - (1870-1950) The last of the great *lionnes comiques*; her remembered song is 'Are we to part like this, Bill?' - The Army

Katherine Docks - Thomas Telford built them in 1828: closed and gentrified in 1968 - Socks

Keystone cop - Series of Mack Sennett films in the 1910s - Chop (of meat)

Khyber Pass - The way into Afghanistan from Pakistan. Treaty of Gandamak, 1879, put it under British control - Arse *"That Fred needs a good kick up the Khyber."*

Kick and prance – Dance

Kidney pie - Eye

Kidney punch - Lunch *"Let's meet for a bit of kidney."*

Kilkenny cats - Felines who had such a fight that only their tails survived - Scats *"Whenever Fred gets excited, he throws his arms around and goes right Kilkenny."*

King Canute's - (955-1035) Danish king of England remembered for telling his syncophantic courtiers that even he could not hold back the tide - Boots

King Dickie - The last King Richard was III, who was killed in 1485 – Brickie (Bricklayer)

King Lear - The over-daughtered monarch in Shakespeare's tragedy - Ear

King's Head - Generally depicted on inn signs as that of Charles I - Shed

King's Proctor - The King's [or Queen's] Proctor is an official with the right to intervene in probate, divorce and nullity cases when collusion or suppression of facts is alleged - Doctor

Kings and Queens - Beans *"I'll have some kings on holy ghost."*

Kingdom come - 'Thy Kingdom come, thy will be done...' Part of the Lord's Prayer - Rum

Kipper and bloater - Motor car / Photo

Kipper and Plaice - Face *"'E's got a kipper like the back of a tram."*

Kiss and cuddle - Muddle, confusion

Kitchen range - Change *"I've got no kitchen, can you cope with a cock and hen?"*

Kitchen stoves - Cloves

Knife and fork - Pork

Knotty Ash - A mythical district in Liverpool, made famous by comedian Ken Dodd - Cash

La-Di-Da - Star - *The Star*, together with the *Evening News* and the *Evening Standard*, was a London evening newspaper in the 1930-1960 period - *"I used to sell the old la-di when I was a lad."* / Car (used when only the upper classes had cars) / Cigar *"The boss smoked a fat la-di-da."*

Lace curtain - Burton beer - Brewed in Burton on Trent

Lady Godiva - (d. 1067) Wife of Leofric, earl of Mercia. Endowed monasteries at Stow and Coventry. In legend, rode naked through Coventry on a white horse. There was a procession in her name held annually in Coventry from 1678 to 1887 - Fiver

Lady Isobel - Isobel Barnet, a television personality mainly on game shows, in the 1950s and 1960s *see* Barnet *"Will you comb your Lady Isobel this instant!"*

Lakes of Killarney - Tourist attraction in County Kerry, Ireland - Barmey *"In my opinion, Fred is Lakes."*

Lambeth Walk - Market in south London. Also song from 1937 musical *Me and My Gal* – Billiard chalk

Lancashire lasses - Spectacles

Last card in the pack - Sack *"Poor old Fred's been given the Last Card again."*

Laugh and joke - Smoke

Laugh and titter - Bitter

Laughs and smiles - Piles

Lean and linger - Finger

Lean and lurch - Church

Left and right - Fight

Lemon and lime - Time

Lemon drop - Cop

Liffey Water - The river rising in the Wicklow Mountains and reaching the sea at Dublin (where Guinness is brewed) - Porter, now all kinds of beer especially Guinness

Light and dark - Park

Lilley and Skinner - A chain of shoe shops - Dinner / Beginner

Lillian Gish - (1896-1993) Born Lillian de Guiche. Film actress, who made her name in *The Birth of a Nation* in 1915 - Fish

Limehouse Cut - Short canal linking the Regent's Canal to the Lee Navigation - Gut *"Fred's getting a bit of a Limehouse on him, ain't he?"*

Linen draper - Newspaper *"Can I borrer yer linen for a mo', please?"*

Lion's lair - Share

Lions roar(ing) - Snore, snoring

Little Boy Blue - 'Little Boy Blue, come blow on your horn...' Nursery rhyme - Screw (prison officer)

Little Brown Jug - 19th century song - Bath plug / Electric plug

Little Nell - Suffering heroine in Dickens' *Old Curiosity Shop* (1841) - Doorbell *"Go on, ring the Little Nell – and run!"*

Little Red Riding Hoods - Tale by Charles Perrault - Stolen goods *"Them little red ridings need to be shifted off this manor sharpish."*

Little Titch - Stage name of Harry Relph (1868-1928), comedian, noted for his big boots and eccentric dancing - Itch

Lloyd's List - Newspaper for the shipping and insurance industry - Pissed *"Arsenal lost, so Fred got Lloyd's."*

Load of hay - Day

Loaf of bread - Head *"Why doesn't Fred ever use his loaf?"*

Lollipop - Drop (gratuity or tip) *"When he's a waiter Fred does well on lollipops."* / Shop (to inform on someone)

Lollipop stick - Quick / Trick

London fog - Dog

Londonderry - Hilly county in Ulster. In the 17th century much of the land was confiscated from its Irish owners and the city was granted to the City Companies of London - Sherry

Longacre - Street running between St Martin's Lane and Drury Lane that derives its name from part of the seven-acre field that was in Covent Garden - Baker

Loop the loop – Aeronatical manoeuvre - Soup *"After the loop, I'll 'ave the Lillian, please."*

Lord Hill - During WWII Charles Hill was the 'Radio Doctor'. Member of Parliament for Luton 1950-63 - Pill

Lord Lovell - A supporter of Richard III, who also fought for Lambert Simnel - Shovel

Lord Mayor - The first Lord Mayor London was appointed in 1189 - Swear *"Stop it. You ain't Lord Mayorin' in 'ere."*

Lord of the Manor - Tanner - Sixpence

Lorna Doone - Novel (1869) by Richard Dodderidge Blackmore - Spoon

Lost and found - Pound - coin or, earlier, note

Love one another - Mother

Lucky dips - Chips

Lucy Lockit(s) - One of the heroines in *The Beggar's Opera* by John Gay - Pocket(s)

Macaroni - A foppish young man mid-18th century. Also a pasta - Pony - Slang for twenty-five pounds

Macaroon - Coon

Madam de Luce - Spruce *"Don't come the old Madam with me, me lad!"*

Madame Tussaud - Waxworks founded in 1802 by Marie Tussaud (1760-1850), now in Marylebone Road - Bald

Mae West - (1892-1980) American film star, Hollywood's original sex symbol - Breast

Mahatma Gandhi - (1869-1948) Statesman, the leader of Indian independence - Brandy

Maidstone jailer - The prison, which used to specialise in printing, is in the county town of Kent - Tailor

Man and wife - Knife

Man o'war - Bore *"That Fred's a right man o'war when it comes to his football hooligan stories."*

Mangle and wringer - Singer

Manhole cover - Brother *"'Ave you met me manhole, Sid?"*

Marble Arch - John Nash's take of the Arch of Constantine in Rome, erected in 1827 near Buckingham Palace and moved to Hyde Park in 1851 - Starch

Margaret Rose - The younger sister of Queen Elizabeth II - Nose

Margate Sands - Popular seaside resort on the Isle of Thanet in Kent - Hands

Maria Monk - A pornographic novel of 1836 was called *The Awful Disclosures of Maria Monk* - Spunk *"Tracey's a looker – and she's got plenty of Maria."*

Marie Corelli Pseudonym of Mary Mackay (1855-1924) who published her first novel in 1886 and achieved fame with *Barabbas* in 1893 - Telly (television set)

Mars bar - A caramel/chocolate sweet – Scar

Mary Ellens - 'I'm shy, Mary Ellen, I'm shy' music hall song – Melons (breasts) *"That Cynthia's got a wonderful pair of Mary Ellens."*

Mary Malone - 'Phone

Max Miller - (1895-1963) Popular music hall and radio comedian - Pillow

Meat pie - Fly (insect) / (trousers) *"Do your meat pie up this instant, Fred!"*

Merry and bright(s) - Light(s)

Merry go round - Pound (currency)

Merry Old Soul - Old King Cole was a merry old soul and a legendary English King, perhaps father of St Helena and the person after whom Colchester was named - Hole

Micky Mouse - Cartoon character created by Walt Disney (1901-66), first appearing in *Steamboat Willie* in 1928 - House

Mile End - A street in Stepney, east London. The site of a Roman castra on the road to Camulodum (Colchester) - Friend

Milkman's horse - Cross *"To say that Fred was milkman's don't really tell you how angry he was!"*

Mince pie(s) - Eye(s)

Miss Fitch - Bitch

Mix and muddle - Cuddle

Moby Dick - A novel (1850) by Herman Melville about a white whale and his pursuer - Nick (prison) / Prick / Sick *"Fred's on the Moby."*

Molly Malone - In the 19th century ballad, she 'wheeled her wheelbarrow through streets broad and narrow singing, "Cockles and mussels, alive, alive-o!"' – 'Phone

Montezumas - (1466-1529) Aztec emperor - Bloomers

Moody and Sankey - Dwight Lyman Moody (1837-99) and David Sankey (1840-1908) compiled the *M & S Hymn Book* in 1873 - Hanky Panky *"Fred gave me a lot of ol' moody about the Mickey."*

More or less - Dress

Moriarty - Sherlock Holmes' adversary - Party

Morris Minor - Popular car model - Shiner *"Have you seen Fred's eye? It's a proper Morris Minor."*

Mother and daughter - Water

Mother Hubbard – In 1805 Sarah Catherine Martin wrote about the woman who tries to placate her hungry dog, but the tale dates from 1591 in a poem by Edmund Spenser - Cupboard

Mother-in-law - Saw (carpenter's)

Mother Kelly - 'On Mother Kelly's doorstep' was a music hall song sung by G H Eliot - Jelly / Telly (television set)

Mother of Pearl - The pearly, iridescent internal layer of some molluscs, used to make decorative objects. Properly called nacre - Girl

Mother's Pride - A brand name for bread - Bride

Mountain passes - Spectacles

Mud in your eye - Tie

Muffin baker - Quaker - A member of the Society of Friends, founded by George Fox in 1647. They got the name in 1650 from Justice Bennet of Derby bidding them 'Tremble at the name of the Lord.'

Muffin the Mule - Television puppet of the 1950s - Fool *"That Fred's a right muffin."*

Mum and dad – Mad

Mumble and mutter - Butter

Mums and dads - Cricket pads

Mustard pickle - Cripple

Mutt and Jeff - The first daily strip cartoon characters, created by Bud Fisher for the *San Francisco Chronicle* in 1907 - Deaf *"You'll 'ave to shout, the poor old dog's mutt."*

Mutter and stutter - Butter

Nancy Lea - Tea

Nanny goat - Boat / Coat *"Ma, 'ave you seen me nanny?"* / Throat *"Fred's on the Moby wiv a sore nanny."* / Tote

National Debt - In Britain incepted on 15 December, 1692 by Charles Montagu, Earl of Halifax, when £1M was secured. This had risen to £20M in 1697; £243M in 1798; £798M in 1903, and £34,194M by 1968 - Bet

Near and far - Bar

Ned Kelly - (1855-80) Australian bushranger, who headed a four-man gang raiding banks in New South Wales. Hanged - Belly

Neddle and cotton - Rotten

Needle and pin - Gin *"... and Freda'll 'ave a drop of needle."* / Thin

Needle and thread - Bread

Nell Gwyn - (1650-87) actress and mistress of Charles II: one of her sons by the king was created Duke of St Albans - Gin

Nellie Bly's - Pseudonym of American journalist Elizabeth Cochrane Seaman (1867-1922) who completed a circuit of the globe in 72 days, six hours and eleven minutes in 1889: popular songs written about her at the time - Thighs *"That Freda's got a lovely pair of Nellies on her."*

Nellie Deans - 'There's an old mill by the stream, Nellie Dean...' music hall song - Greens (vegetables)

Nelson Eddy's - The co-star with Jeannette Macdonald of many a film musical in the 1930s, most memorably *Rose Marie* - Readies *"I'd love to settle up today, but I've got no Nelsons on me."*

Neptune's daughter - Neptune was the Roman God of the Sea, represented by an old gentleman carrying a trident - Water

Nervo and Knox - Jimmy Nervo (1890-1975) and Teddy Knox (1896-1974), music hall comedians and members of the Crazy Gang - Goggle box (television)

Nervous wreck - Cheque *"I've not had the nervous from the beggarme this week."*

Never fear - Beer

Newington Butts - A Southwark street running between Elephant and Castle and Kennington - Guts

Niagara Falls - Spectacular cataract on the Niagara River between Lakes Erie and Ontario. The American Falls are 167 feet high, while the Canadian or Horseshoe Falls are 158 feet high. A popular honeymoon destination for Americans - Stalls

Night and day - Grey *"You'll nag me 'til I'm night 'n' day."* / Play

Nits and lice - Starting price

Noah's Ark - The vessel built to escape the Biblical Flood, reported in Genesis, 5-9 - Dark (no light) / Nark (informant)

North and south - Mouth

Nose and chin - Win

Nose bleeder - Reader

Nova Scotia - Discovered by John Cabot in 1497; colonised by the French 1598, taken by the English 1614. Back to France 1667, English again 1689, French 1697, English 1710. A Canadian province - Kosher - Hebrew-Yiddish meaning 'clean to eat'.

Nursery rhyme - Crime

Oats and barley - Charley *"Fred's a right oats."*

Ocean pearl - Girl

Ocean wave - Shave

Oily rag - Fag (cigarette) *"'Ere, Fred, got any oilys?"*

Old Folks at Home - A sentimental song by Stephen Collins Foster (1826-64) - Comb *"I think your Barnet could use an Old Folks."*

Old oak - Smoke (the Smoke, nickname for London)

Oliver Twist - A novel (1837) by Charles Dickens about an orphan trapped by the London underworld - Fist

On the floor - Poor

Once a week - Beak (magistrate) / Cheek (impudence)

One and t'other - Brother / Mother

One for his nob - A score of a single point in cribbage for having the jack of the leading suit in the hand - Bob (shilling)

Orange pip - Japanese

Orchestra stalls – Balls *"He's a chicken with no orchestras."*

Oscar Asche - (1871-1936) Australian actor-manager, renowned for producing and acting in *Chu-Chin-Chow* during the Great War - Cash

Oscar Slater's - Convicted of murder in Glasgow in 1909. Conan Doyle believed in his innocence and proved that another man had done the crime; Slater was released in 1927 - Potatoes *"Jim serves up some good baked Oscars on his stall."*

Overcoat maker - Undertaker

Owen Nares - (1888-1943) Shakespearean actor - Chairs

Oxford scholar - Dollar - When this term was first used there were generally four dollars to the pound sterling, hence an Oxford was worth five shillings

Oxo Cube - Originally Liebig's meat extract - Tube (London underground)

Ps and Qs - To take care to observe polite social conventions in one's speech and manner. Variously, ps and qs are meant to represent pints and quarts, please and thank-you, to stop children mixing up the p and q opposite-facing letters, or, from the French, *pieds* and *queues* - dance instructions - Shoes

Paddy and Mick - Pickaxe / Thick

Paddy Quick - Stick / Thick (Stupid)

Pair of braces - Horse races

Pair of kippers - Slippers

Pall Mall - The London street of clubs and palaces. In the 17th century it was the home of the Westminster coffee houses - Gal

Park Lane - Fashionable street to the east of Hyde Park - Pain / Plain *"Gawd, Fred's new Pall ain't 'arf Park!"*

Pastry cook - Book *"Our Kev's got more pastries than the bleedin' lib'ry."*

Pearly Gate - *Revelations 21:21* refers to 'The twelve gates were twelve pearls'. A hymn by Isaac Watts (1674-1748) brings them to modern readers - Plate

Peas in the pot - Hot

Peckham Rye - South of Peckham, south London, is Peckham Rye and Peckham Rye Common - Tie *"'ave you seen Fred's flashy new Peckham?"*

Pen and ink - Stink *"'Ere, Mick, put some disinfectant down the bog, it don't 'arf pen in there."*

Penny a Mile - In 1844 railways were required by law to run at least one train daily over each line at a minimum speed of 12 miles per hour, including stops at every station, at fares not exceeding one penny a mile. Known as the Parliamentary Trains, some companies ran them at very unsocial hours or with frequent shunting out of the way for faster through trains - Smile *"Cheer up, an' give us a penny, darlin'."*

Penny a pound - Ground - the race track

Penny for the Guy - Demand by children in early November recalling the Gunpowder Plot (1605) and Guy Fawkes (1570-1606) - Pie

Peter Pan - The boy who never grew up in a play by Sir J M Barrie in 1904. Peter Pan's statue in Kensington Gardens was placed there in 1912 – Van *"Fred's got a new Peter Pan."*

Petticoat Lane - Street market in Middlesex Street, Stepney – Pain *"I've got a right Petticoat in me guts."*

Photo finish - Guinness *"Give 'im a foater, Jim."*

Piccadilly - Fashionable London street from Hyde Park to Piccadilly Circus, named after Pickadilly Hall, itself derived from piccadil - a decorative border inserted on the edge of an article of dress - Silly

Pick and choose - Booze

Pickled pork - Chalk

Pie and mash - Flash / Slash *"I'm bustin for a pie and mash!"*

Pig and roast - Toast

Pig's ear - Beer *"Pint of pigs, please, Doris."*

Pig's face - Lace

Pig's trotter - Squatter

Pillar and post - Originally referred to the movement of the ball in Real Tennis - Ghost *"Struth, you look like you've seen a pillar!"*

Pimple and blotch - Scotch

Pint pot - Sot *"Fred's a drunk, but Phil's a pint pot."*

Pipe and drum - Bum

Pitch and toss - A game in which the player who comes closest to hitting a mark with a coin is entitled to toss all the other coins and keep those that land head up - Boss *"Look out, pitch about!"*

Plate of ham - Tram - Horse-drawn trams were introduced in London in 1870

Plates and dishes - Kisses / Missus

Plates of meat - Feet *"These Ps an' Qs ain't 'arf 'urting me plates."* / Street

Pleasure and pain - Rain

Plymouth Argyll - Football team - File

Plymouth Sound - Between the Plym and Tamar Estuaries, long important as a naval station. Sir Francis Drake and, later, the *Mayflower* figure in its history - Pound (currency)

Polly Flinder - 'Little Polly Flinders sat among the cinders.' Nursery rhyme - Window

Polly Parrot - Carrot

Pontypool - In the South Wales coalfield, Pontypool began smelting iron in 1577 and was an early centre for tinplate - School *"Learn anything at Ponty today, Wayne?"*

Pony and trap - Crap *"Don't you give me none of that old pony!"*

Pope of Rome – Home *"I'll be ready waiting when you're Pope."*

Pork chop - Cop

Pork pies - Lies *"Blimey, Fred does tell a good porkey, dun't 'e?"*

Postman's knock - Children's kissing game - Clock

Pot and pan - Man *"'Ave you met me old pot and pan?"*

Pot of glue - Queue

Pot of honey - Money *"He's got pots."*

Pot of jelly - Belly

Potatoes in the mould - Cold *"It's bleedin' 'taters in here."*

Pots and dishes - Wishes
Pound of butter - Nutter
Pride and joy - Boy
Pudding and gravy - Navy *"Bert's joined the pudding."*
Pudding chef - Deaf

Puff and dart - Start   *"If only Fred'd make a puff and dart on that shelvin'."*

Punch and Judy - The children's puppet show introduced into England from Italy about 1660 - Moody

Put and take - A game of chance with dice mark on each side, the winner to 'take' the pot - Cake

Put in the boot - Shoot

Quaker Oat - Not the correct name for the Society of Friends, but a breakfast cereal - Coat

Quarter to two - Jew

Queen of the South - Edinburgh football team - Mouth

Queen's Park Rangers - Hammersmith, west London, football team, located in Loftus Road since 1917 - Strangers

Quiver and shake - Steak

Rabbit and pork - Talk   *"All them Councillors ain't nuthin' but rabbit, if you ask me."*

Rabbit hutch - Crutch

Radio Rental - High Street chain of shops – Mental   *"When I told 'im, 'e went completely Radio Rental."*

Rag and bone - Throne (lavatory)

Rangoon - City in Myanmar [Burma] - Prune

Rank and riches - Britches

Raspberry tart - Fart   *"Fred blew that referee such a raspberry."*

Rat and mouse - House

Rattle and clank - Bank

Rats and mice - Dice

Rattlesnakes - The shakes

Raw and ripe - Pipe

Rawalpindi - City in the Punjab in the foothills of the Himalayas. A major British military outpost from 1849 -   Windy

Read and write - Fight / Flight

Red, white and blue - Shoe

Reeling and rocking - Stocking

Reels of cotton - Rotten

Richard the Third - (1452-85). The last Plantagenet king of England. Slain at the Battle of Bosworth. Possibly the killer of the Princes in the Tower - Turd   *"Is it your dog wot left that Richard in the kitchen?"*

Riddle-me-ree - Means 'answer me this puzzle', short for riddle me this riddle - Pee

Riff-raff - The dregs of humanity - Taff (Welshman) - From *Dafydd*, a common name in Wales

Rifle range - Change

Rinky-dink - Pink *"Fred's in the rinky-dink since his holiday in Ibiza."*

Rip and tear - Swear

Rip Van Winkle - The hero of Washington Irving's story (1820) - Tinkle *"Fred just popped out for a Rip."*

Rise and shine - Wine

River Lea - Waterway marking the border between Essex and Hertfordshire - Tea

River Nile - The Blue and White Niles constitute the longest river in Africa - Smile

Roast beef - The French call the British *les Rosbifs* - Teeth

Roast pork - Fork

Rob Roy - Born Robert McGregor (1671-1734). Scottish clan chief and cattle dealer. Sir Walter Scott's novel (1818) was based on his exploits - Boy

Robin Hood - Traditional outlaw hero, first mentioned in *Piers Plowman* by Langland in 1377. Wynkyn de Worde (the second English printer) published *A Lytell Geste of Robyn Hode* in 1489. Generally located in Nottingham Forest, although Barnsdale, Yorkshire, is also a haunt. Period from Richard I (1189-99) to Edward II (1307-27) - Good

Robinson and Cleaver - A now-closed London department store - Fever *"Wayne's in bed with a Robinson."*

Rock of Ages - The well-known hymn, *Rock of Ages, cleft for me*, was written in 1775 by Augustus Montague Toplady - Wages

Rocks and boulders - Shoulders

Rogue and villain - Shilling

Roll me in the gutter - Butter

Rolling billows - Pillows

Rolls Royce - The motor car company was established by Charles Stewart Rolls (1877-1910) and Frederick Henry Royce (1863-1933) – Voice *"I've lorst me Rolls since last Sat'day at Millwall."*

Rookery Nook - Aldwych farce by Ben Travers (1926) - Book

Rose buds - Spuds

Rory O'Moore - Door *"Show the gent the Rory now, if he don't mind, Justin."*

Rosie Lee - Gipsy Rose Lee (1914-70), American strip-tease artist of international reputation. Real name Rose Louise Hovick - Tea *"They do a good cuppa Rosie down Ernie's caff."*

Rosie O'Grady's - From the 1943 film starring Betty Grable - Ladies *"Sylv's just gone to the Rosie, she'll only be a minute."*

Rotten Row - The equestrian track in the south of Hyde Park, London, said to get its name from *route de roi* - Blow

Round the houses - Trousers *"That's a smashin' pair of round-mys, Fred."*

Rowton Houses - Lodging houses for working men established by Montagu Lowry (Lord Rowton) in 1892 - Trousers

Roy Rodgers - (1912-98) American film cowboy - Bodgers *"Don't give no buildin' work to that Fred, he's just a Roy Rodger."*

Rub a dub - Rub-a-dub-dub, three men in a tub - nursery rhyme - Pub *"See yer down the rub a dub later?"*

Ruby Murray - (1935-96) An Irish vocalist. Got five singles in the Top Twenty in one week in 1955 - Curry

Rudolph Hess - (1894-1987) Deputy Leader of the Nazi Party in Germany - Mess

Rupert Bears - Children's cartoon character devised for the *Daily Express* by Mary Tourtel in 1920 - Shares *"Adrian's got on well in the City and now he's dealing in Ruperts."*

Sacks of rice - Mice

Sad and sorry - Lorry

Safe and sound - Ground *"Fred fell off 'is ladder and landed flat on the safe and sound."*

Salmon and trout - Gout *"Fred's sufferin' from the salmon this month."* / Snout (snuff)

Salvation Army – Religious body founded in 1865 by William Booth - Barmey

Sammy Halls - *Me name is Samuel Hall*, melodramatic music hall song created by W G Ross - Balls

Samuel Pepys - (1633-1703) Diarist and Secretary to the Naval Office - The creeps *"That Jason gives me the Samuel Pepys."*

Sandy McNab - Cab

Sarah Gamp - A character in Charles Dickens' *Martin Chuzzlewit*. Her large cotton umbrella has given the name 'gamp' to all blowsy umbrellas - Lamp

Satin and lace - Face

Saucepan lid - Quid (£) / Kid *"'Ow many saucepans has that Gladys got now?"* / Con or deceive *"Would I saucepan you?"*

Sausage and mash - Cash *"Now's the time to tap Fred - he's in the sausage today."*

Sausage roll - Dole

Scapa Flow - A waterway in the Orkney Islands, where, on 21st June, 1919, Admiral Reuter scuttled the interned German fleet - Go *"You'd better scarper smartish."*

Scotch eggs - Legs

Scrap metal - Kettle

Screwdriver - Skiver (avoids work)

Semolina - Cleaner (charwoman)

Seven and six - Fix *"I'll seven and six that in a brace of shakes."*

Sexton Blake - Fictional detective, whose stories lack violence, sor romance, aimed at the juvenile market. The character was probably created by John G Brandon (1879-1941), but was by many hands in the *Sexton Blake Library*, a fortnightly periodical issued by Amalgamated Press - Cake / Fake (forgery) / Steak

Shake and shiver - River

Shepherd's pie - Minced lamb with potato topping - Sky

Shepherd's plaid - Bad

Sherbert dab - Cab

Shillings and pence - Sense

Shiny and bright - All right

Ship in full sail - Ale

Shirt and collar - Dollar

Shiver and shake - Slice of cake *"Can I have a shiver to go wiv me Rosie, Gladys?"*

Shout and holler - Dollar

Shovels and spades - AIDS

Shower bath - Ten shillings (half a pound) *"I'll give yer showers to a tanner that Fred falls off that ladder."*

Silent Night - Christmas carol composed in Austria - Light ale

Silver and gold - Old

Simple Simon - Gormless nursery rhyme character, who met a pie-man - Diamond

Sinbad the Sailor - Seven stories in *The Arabian Nights' Entertainments* concern Sinbad, a wealthy citizen of Baghdad, who voyaged on various adventures - Tailor *"That Kangar is the best Sinbad round 'ere."*

Sir Walter Scott - (1771-1832) Scottish novelist and poet - Pot of beer

Sit beside her - Little Miss Muffet Sat on a tuffet, Eating her curds and whey; There came a big spider... the rest is history. Nursery rhyme - Spider

Six and eight - State (upset, agitated) / Straight (trustworthy)

Six months' hard - Prison sentence - Bingo card

Six to four - Whore

Skin and blister - Sister

Sky diver - Fiver

Skylark – Traditional name for pleasure boat - Park a car *"Effie'll be about half an hour, she's trying to skylark her kipper."*

Skyrocket - Pocket

Skyscraper - The Equitable Life Assurance Society building was erected in New York in 1868, made possible by bed-rock foundations and high-speed passenger lifts. For many years after its erection in 1930-32, the Empire State Building in New York was the world's tallest skyscraper - Paper (all types)

Slap and tickle - Pickle (to eat)

Slice of toast - Ghost

Slither and dodge - Freemasonry lodge *"Fred rolled up his trouser and went down the slither."*

Slug and snail - Fingernail

Smash and grab - Taxi-cab

Smile and smirk - Work

Smoked haddock - Racing paddock

Smooth and coarse - Horse

Snake in the grass - Looking glass

Sniffer and snorter - Newspaper reporter

Snoop and pry - Cry

Snoozing and snoring - Boring

Snow and ice - Price (cost) / Starting price (racing)

Snow Whites - Snow White is a traditional fairy story about a girl, her wicked step-mother, seven dwarfs, and a handsome prince. Made into a cartoon film by Walt Disney in 1937 – Tights *"She's wearing black Snow Whites for a bet."*

Soaks - Folks

Soap and flannel - The panel *"Fred's on the soap with the doctor again."*

Soap and lather - Father

Soap and water - Daughter

Sodom and Gomorrah - The cities of the Plain overwhelmed as Mrs Lot turned round – Borrow *"Fred only Sodomed your barrer – it'll be back termorrer."*

Soldier ants - Pants *"Don't get your soldiers in a twist, squire."*

Soldier Bold - 'Ben Battle was a soldier bold, And used to war's alarms: But a cannon-ball took off his legs, So he laid down his arms!' Thomas Hood (1799-1845) - Cold *"Old Fred's got a nasty soldier."*

Song and dance - Chance *"Any song an' dance of a loan, Sid?"*
Song of the thrush - Brush / Broom
Songs and sighs - Thighs
Sorry and sad - Bad / Dad
Sorrowful tale - Jail
Soup and gravy - The Navy
South of France - Dance
Southend on Sea – South Essex day trip destination - Pee
Southend Pier - The longest pleasure pier in the world, founded in 1829 - Ear
Spanish Main - Central and South American coast from Panama to the Orinoco River - Drain *"Fred's got his arm caught down the Spanish."*
Spanish waiter - Pre-dates *Fawlty Towers'* Manuel by many years - Potato
Spare rib - Fib
Spit and drag - Fag (cigarette)
Split asunder - Costermonger
Sporting Life - Racing newspaper - Wife
Spotted dick - Sick
Squabbling bleeder - Squadron Leader (R.A.F.)
Stammer and stutter - Butter
Stan and Ollie - Stan Laurel (1890-1965) and Oliver Hardy (1892- 1957) Hollywood comedians - Brollie (Umbrella)
Stand at ease - Cheese / Freeze

Stand to attention - Pension
Steam packet - Jacket
Steam tug - Mug *"That Fred's a right steam tug."*
Steamroller - Bowler hat
Stephenson's Rocket - The railway engine invented by George Stephenson (1781-1848) - Pocket
Stewed prune - Tune
Sticks and stones - Bones
Sticky bun - Son
Sticky toffee - Coffee
Stop and go - Toe
Stop and start - Heart
Storm and strife - Wife
Strawberry tart - Heart *"He made me strawberry go all of a dither."*
String beans - Jeans
String vest - Pest *"That Fred's always nagging, he's a right string vest."*
Struggle and strain - Train (exercise)
Struggle and strife - Life / Wife
Strugglers and strainers - Trainers *"Young Kevin needs some new strugglers."*
Sugar and honey - Money
Sugar and spice - Nice
Sugar candy - Brandy / Handy (sarcastic) *"This bucket wivout a 'andle is very sugar candy."*
Sunday best - Vest
Swallow and sigh - Collar and Tie
Swan Lake - Ballet with music by P I Tchaikovski - Cake *"I'll 'ave a nice piece of Swan, Flossie."*
Swanee River - River rising in the Okefenoee swamp in southeast Georgia and flowing 250 miles to the Gulf of Mexico in Florida. Epitomises the poor American south in song - Liver
Swear and cuss - Bus *"The laughin' swear's late again."*
Sweeney Todd - The Demon Barber of Fleet Street created in a play by George Dibdin Pitt (1799-1855) - Flying Squad
Syrup of fig(s) - Laxative medicine, particularly dosed to children - Wig(s) *"Fred's syrup don't fit!"*
Tapioca - Joker (in cards)
Tar and feather - Stripped to the buff, daubed with tar, then rolled in feathers: a popular punishment for cheats - The weather
Tartan banner - Tanner (Sixpence)
Tate and Lyle - Sugar manufacturers, chaired first by Sir Henry

Tate (1819-99), later by Sir Charles Ernest Leonard Lyle (1882-1954) - Style *"Jim's got a bit of Tate and Lyle about 'im."*

Tea and Toast - Post. *"Only got bills in the tea and toast, as per usual."* / Winning Post *"Arfur's not going to get that nag past the tea and toast in a million years."*

Tea leaf - Thief

Teapot lid - Kid / Yid

Teddy Bear - Popular cuddly toy named after American President Theodore Roosevelt (1858-1919) – Pear

Tellytubby - Children's television character – Hubby *"'Ve you met me second tellytubby – Wayne?"*

Terrible Turk - Work

These and those - Clothes / Toes

Theydon Bois - Essex commuter town, near Epping - Noise

Thick and thin - Chin / Gin

Thimble and thumb - Rum

This and that - Bat (cricket) / Flat / Hat

Thistledown - Pissing down *"Today's right thistledown."*

Thomas Cook - (1808-92) Pioneer travel agent - Look *"Did you see the Thomas Cook wot she give 'im?"*

Thomas Tilling - Omnibus proprietor based in south London from 1847. His fifteen-minute service to the City was described by a conductor as 'A quarter arter, 'alf arter, quarter to and at.' - Shilling

Thousand pities - Titties

Three Blind Mice - A farmer's wife de-tailed them in the nursery rhyme - Rice

Threepenny bits - A pre-decimal coin - Tits *"Don't 'h just get on yer threepenny bits?"*

Thyme and borage - Porridge - In vulgar parlance, being sent to prison is being given 'time'.

Tickle your fancy - Nancy *"That Cedric is a right Tickle."*

Tiddler's bait - Late

Tiddley wink - A game in which players try to snap small counters into a cup by pressing them on the edge with a larger counter - Drink *"Fred went on the tiddley last week."*

Tilbury Docks - South Essex port opened in 1886 - Socks

Tin bath - Scarf

Tin tack - Sack *"Fred's got the tin tack again!"*

Tin tacks - Facts

Tin tank - Bank

Tit for tat - Hat *"It's cold. Put yer titfer on yer crust."*

Tit willow - 'On a tree by a river a little tom-tit Sang 'Willow, titwillow, titwillow!'' Song from *The Mikado* by W S Gilbert - Pillow

Toby jug - Mug

To and fro - Snow *"It's bleedin' cold enuff to to and fro."*

Toad in the hole - Roll of notes

Toasted bread - Dead *"Did yer 'ear Max's dad's toasted."*

Tod Sloane - (1873-1933) American jockey - Alone *"You on yer Tod tonight, Mavis?"*

Toffee wrapper - Napper (head)

Toilet roll - Dole

Tom and Dick - Sick (usually not serious)

Tom Sawyer - Character used in a pair of folksy novels by Mark Twain (1835-1910) - Lawyer (in the legal profession or a 'know it all') *"Fred's a right Tom when it comes to 'is rights."*

Tom Thumb - In legend, the son of a ploughman in the days of King Arthur. He was as tall as his father's thumb and had many absurd adventures – swallowed by a cow, carried off by a raven, and swallowed by Giant Grumbo. More recently, 'General Tom Thumb' (real name Charles Sherwood Stratton (1838-83)) grew to 25 inches tall and was exhibited in Europe and America - Rum

Tom Tit - Male blue tit - Shit *"I could do with a Tom Tit."*

Tomato sauce - Horse

Tomfoolery - Tom Fool is either mentally deficient or acts the part of one who is. Proverb - More know Tom Fool than Tom Fool knows - Jewellery

Tommy Dodd - The Tommy Dodd is one who, in tossing up, either wins or loses, according to an agreement with a confederate – Odd

Tommy Trinder - (1909-89) English comedian - Window

Tommy Tucker - Master Tucker sang for his supper in the nursery rhyme - Supper

Tomorrow - Borrow *"Look away, boys, Fred's on the tommy again."*

Tooting Bec - An ancient Manor of Streatham held by the Abbot of St Mary de Bec in 1086 - Peck *"All friends again? Come on, give us a Tooting."*

Top hat – Invented in Florence aeound 1760, but generally adopted in the 1830s. Made of polished beaver, but later fashioned of plush. - Prat / Rat

Top joint - Pint of beer

Total wreck - Cheque

Tower Bridge - Built in 1894 in the Gothic style, this Thames crossing is sited beside the Tower of London. It has bascules that lift to allow tall ships into the Pool of London - Fridge *"Put the pig's ear in the tower to cool."*

Town Crier - Liar

Trafalgar Square - Named after the 1805 sea battle: it features a memorial to Horatio Nelson (1758-1805) - Chair

Trombone - 'Phone *"That Cynthia's never off the trombone."*

Treble chance - Dance

Trolley and tram - Ham

Trouble and fuss - Bus

Trouble and strife - Wife *"I'd better be off, the trouble was expecting me 'ome 'alf an hour ago."*

Troubles and cares - Stairs

Trunk and tree - Knee

Tug o'war - Game of strength between two teams pulling on a rope - Whore

Tumble down the sink - Drink *"Fancy another tumble?"*

Turkish bath - A steam bath inducing heavy perspiration – Laugh

Turkish delight - Gelatinous sweet cut into cubes and drenched in icing sugar - Tight

Turtle dove(s) – *Streptopelia turtur* - Gloves *"Got yer turtles, Fred? We don't want to leave no dabs."* / Love

Twists and twirls - Girls

Two and eight - State *"When she was pulled over by the fuzz she was in a right two and eight."*

Two bob bits – A florin, worth two shillings, now ten pence – Shits *"That roller-coaster ride gave Fred the two bobs."*

Two thirty - Dirty *"How you can get so two thirty when you're just supposed to be in the choir, I will never know."*

Typewriter - At the end of the 19th century a typewriter was the person (generally female) who operated a typewriting machine - Fighter

Ugly Sister - One of a pair of characters in the pantomime *Cinderella* - Blister

Umbrella - Fellow *"'Ave you met me umbrella?"*

Uncle Bert - Shirt (to wear)

Uncle Bertie - Shirty (annoyed) *"Don't you get all Uncle Berties with me, mate!"*

Uncle Dick - Sick

Uncle Fred - Bread

Uncle Mac - Donald McCullough, presenter in the 1940s *Children's Hour* on radio - Smack (heroin)

Uncle Ned - Bed

Uncle Sam - National nickname for Americans, derived from Samuel Wilson, who supplied salt pork and beef stamped U.S. to the American Army in the War of 1812 - Lamb

Uncle Wilf - Filth (police)

Uncle Willie - Chilly / Silly

Union Jack – Azure, the Crosses saltire of St Andrew and St Patrick quarterly per saltire counter-charged, argent and gules, the latter fimbriated of the second, surmounted by the Cross of St George of the third fimbriated as the saltire: By order of the Council - Back

Up and under - Thunder

Upper deck - Buses, ships, and piers can have an upper storey - Neck

Upside down - Clown

Uriah Heep - An obsequious character in Charles Dickens' *David Copperfield* - Creep

Vanity Fair - A novel by W M Thackeray published in monthly parts 1847-8 - Chair / Share

Vera Lynn - A London-born vocalist, born 1917, who was the Forces' Sweetheart to British servicemen in World War II - Gin

Vicar of Bray - Song by Anon about a time-serving cleric who boasts he has accommodated himself to the religious views in the reigns of Charles, James, William, Anne and George - Tray

Wanstead Flats - About 400 acres at the south end of Epping Forest. A traditional meeting place for gypsies - Spats *"Fred was turned out nice for the wedding; he was even wearing Wansteads."*

Watch and chain - Brain

Waterloo - The deciding battle in the Napoleonic Wars in 1815 - Stew

Weasel and stoat - Overcoat *"Don't forget yer weasel, it's going to be 'taters tonight."*

Wee Georgie Wood - (1910-60) Diminutive music hall entertainer - **Good** *"Is that new bitter Wee Georgie?"*

Wee Willie Winky - In the nursery rhyme Mr Winky ran through the town in his night attire - Chinkie (Chinese)

Weep and wail - Tale *"That Fred can spin a wonderful weep."*

Weeping willow - Pillow

West Ham Reserves - Football team based at the Boleyn Ground, Upton Park, Newham - Nerves *"You're getting on me West Hams, Gladys."*

Westminster Abbey - Founded by Edward the Confessor in 1060, the church where sovereigns of England and, latterly, the United Kingdom are crowned - Cabby

Whistle and flute - Suit *"That check whistle looks smashin' on you."*

Whistle and toot - Loot

Wicked rumours - Bloomers

Wicked witch - Bitch

Widow Twankey - The hero's 'mother' in the pantomime *Alladin* - Handkerchief

Widow's mite - See Mark xii.42-44 - Light

Wilkie Bard - (1874-1944) Music hall comedian: he sang 'She sells sea shells on the sea-shore...' - Race card

Wilkie Bards - Real name William Augustus Smith; won so many amateur talent competitions that someone said he should be barred – so he re-named himself! - Playing cards

Will o' the wisps - Sponanous methane gas lights appearing in marshy ground, hence ephemeral - Crisps *"... and while you're there, get a packet of wills."*

William Tell - The mythical national hero of Switzerland who defied Albert I, duke of Austria, and, having shot an apple from his son's head, led the fight for Swiss independence - Smell *"Blimey, where's that William Tell comin' from?"*

Win or lose - Booze

Woolly vest - Pest *"That Fred's proposed three times; he's a right woolly vest."*

Woolwich Ferry - The Great Eastern, North London, and London and North-Western Railways ran trains to North Woolwich from where ran steam-ferries to Woolwich Pier on the Kent side – Sherry

Working classes - Spectacles

Yankee Clippers - Sailing ships built for speed of transporting consumables rather than for capacity - Slippers
Yarmouth bloater - Herrings cured on the east coast - Motor
Yellow silk - Milk
Yiddisher fiddle - Diddle
Yorkshire tyke - Radio mike
You and me - Flea / Tea
Yours and ours - Flowers
Yuletide log - Dog

AIDS – Shovels and spades
Ale – Daily Mail / Day and night / Full sail / Silent Night
All right - Shiny and bright
Alone - Darby and Joan / Jack Jones / Tod Sloane
Arm – Chalk Farm
Arms – False alarms
Army – Daft and barmy / Kate Carney
Arse – Aristotle / Bottle and glass / Khyber Pass
Autumn leaf – Thief
Back – Union Jack
Bad – Shepherd's plaid / Sorry and sad
Baker – Longacre
Bald - Madame Tussaud
Balls – Cobblers' awls / Orchestra stalls / Sammy Halls
Banana – Gertie Gitana
Banger – Bernhard Langer
Bank – Arthur Rank / Frank & Hank / Iron tank / Rattle & clank / Tin tank
Bar – Jack Tar / Near and far
Barber – Dover Harbour
Barmey – Lakes of Killarney / Salvation Army
Barrow – Cock sparrow
Basin – Charlie Mason / Fortnum and Mason
Bat – This and that
Bath – Hat and scarf
Batty – Carlo Gatti
Beak – Bubble and squeak
Beans – Kings and Queens
Bed – Uncle Ned
Bedbugs – Hearth rugs
Beer – Charley Freer / Far and near / Lace curtain / Never fear / Pig's ear
Beginner – Lilley and Skinner
Believe – Adam & Eve / Christmas Eve
Belly – Aunt Nelly / Cousin Nellie / Derby Kelly / Ned Kelly / Pot of jelly
Bet – House to let / National Debt
Bike – Clever Mike
Bill – Jack and Jill
Bills – Beecham's pills
Bingo card – Six months' hard

Bitch – Miss Fitch / Wicked Witch
Bitter – Apple fritter / Laugh and titter
Blind – Bacon rind / Golden Hind
Blister – Brother and sister / Ugly Sister
Bloomers – Montezumas / Wicked rumours
Blow – Rotten Row
Boat – All afloat / Hat and coat / Nanny goat
Bodgers – Roy Rodgers
Boil – Conan Doyle
Bollocks – Flowers and frolics
Bombs – Derry and Toms
Bones – Sticks and stones
Book – Captain Cook / /Pastry cook / Rookery Nook
Boots – Daisy roots / King Canute's
Booze – Pick and choose / Win or lose
Bore – Man o'war
Boring – Snoozing and snoring
Borrow – Sodom and Gomorrah / Tomorrow
Boss – Edmundo Ros / Pitch and toss
Bottle – Aristotle
Bouncer – Half ouncer
Bowels – Baden Powells
Bowler hat – Steamroller
Box – Nervo and Knox
Boy – Hobbledehoy / Pride and joy / Rob Roy
Boy Scout – Brussels sprout
Braces – Airs and graces / Epsom races
Brain – Watch and chain
Brains – Down the drains
Brake – Charlie Drake
Brandy – Andy Pandy / Fine and dandy / Jack a Dandy / Mahatma Gandhi / Sugar candy
Brass – Beggar boy's ass
Brat – Jack Sprat
Bread – Needle and thread / Uncle Fred
Breast – Bristol City / Cabman's rest / Mae West
Breasts – Brace and bits / Cat and kitties / Thousand pities / Threepenny bits
Bricklayer – King Dickie
Bride – Mother's Pride
Britches – Rank and riches
Broke – Coal and coke / Hearts of oak
Brokers – Engineers and stokers
Broom – Bride and groom
Brother – Manhole cover / One and t'other
Brown – Camden Town
Brush – Blackbird and thrush / Song of the thrush
Bum – Fife and drum / Jew chum / Pipe and drum
Bus – Swear and cuss / Trouble and fuss
Bus fare – Grey mare
Butter – Cough and splutter / Mumble and mutter / Mutter and stutter / Roll me in the gutter / Stammer and stutter
Cab - Flounder and dab / Sandy McNab / Sherbert dab / Smash and grab
Cabbage – Joe Savage

Cabby – Westminster Abbey
Cadge – Doggett's Coat and Badge
Cake – Give and take / Put and take / Sexton Blake / Shiver and shake / Swan Lake
Candle – Harry Randall / Jack Randall
Cap – Game of Nap
Car – Balloon car / Jam jar / Kipper and bloater / La-Di-Da
Car Park – Copper's nark
Card – Bladder of lard / Wilkie Bard
Cards – Wilkie Bards
Carrot – Polly Parrot
Cash – Bangers and mash / Harry Nash / Knotty Ash / Oscar Asche / Sausage and mash
Cat – Ball of fat
Ceiling – Fellow-feeling
Cell – Flowery dell
Chair – Here and there / Trafalgar Square / Vanity Fair
Chairs – Owen Nares
Chalk – Lambeth Walk / Pickled pork
Chance – Song and dance
Change – Kitchen range / Rifle range
Cheek – Hide and seek
Cheese – Balmy breeze / Bended knees / Cough and sneeze / Flying trapeze / Stand at ease
Cheque – Bushel and peck / Duchess of Teck / Goose's neck / Nervous wreck / Total wreck
Chest – East and west
Chief – Bully beef / Joint of beef
Chill – Frock and frill
Chilly – Uncle Willie
Chin – Errol Flynn / Gunga Din / Thick and thin
Chinese – Wee Willy Winkie
Chips – Lucky dips
Chop – Keystone cop
Church – Lean and lurch
Cinema – Box of tricks
Cleaner – Semolina
Clock – Dickory dock / Postman's knock
Clothes – These and those
Cloudy – Dull and dowdy
Cloves- Kitchen stoves
Clown – Upside down
Clue – Danny la Rue
Coach – Cockroach
Coat – John O'Groat / Nanny goat / Quaker oat
Coffee – Everton toffee
Coffee – Sticky toffee
Cold – Potatoes in the mould / Soldier bold
Collar – Half a dollar
Collar and tie – Swallow and sigh
Comb – Garden gnome / Ideal Home / Old folks at home
Conk – Glass of plonk
Cook – Babbling brook / Beecher's Brook
Coon – Macaroon
Cop – Lemon drop / Pork chop

Copper – Bottle and stopper / Clodhopper / Grasshopper
Corduroy trousers – House of Lords
Cork – Duke of York
Corner – Johnny Horner
Costermonger – Split asunder
Cough – Horse and trough
Cousin – Baker's dozen
Coward – Charlie Howard
Creep – Uriah Heep
Creeps – Samuel Pepys
Crime – Nursery rhyme
Cripple – Mustard pickle
Crisps – Will o'the wisps
Crook – Babbling brook / Joe Hook
Cross – Milkman's horse
Crutch – Rabbit hutch
Cry – Snoop and pry
Cuddle – Mix and muddle
Cupboard – Mother Hubbard
Curry – Ruby Murray
Dance - Kick and prance / South of France / Treble chance
Dark - Noah's Ark
Darts – Horses and carts
Daughter – Bottle of water / Bricks and mortar / Holy water / Soap and water
Dawn – Cape Horn
Day – Load of hat
Dead - Brown bread / Currant bread / Toasted bread
Deaf – Mutt and Jeff / Pudding chef
Deceive – Saucepan lid
Diamond – Simple Simon
Dice – Block of ice / Cats and mice / Rats and mice
Diddle – Yiddisher fiddle
Dinner – Jim Skinner / Lilley and Skinner
Dirty – Two thirty
Dive – Beehive
Dock – Brighton rock
Doctor – Gamble and Proctor / King's Proctor
Dog – Cherry hog / London fog / Yuletide log
Dogs – Golliwogs
Dole – Jam roll / Sausage roll / Toilet roll
Dollar – Oxford scholar / Shirt and collar / Shout and holler
Door – Bobbie Moore / Rory O'Moore
Doorbell – Little Nell
Dope – Bob Hope / Joe Soap
Dozen – Country cousin
Drain – Spanish Main
Draught – George Raft
Drawers – Early doors
Dress – More or less
Drink – Tiddley wink / Tumble down the sink
Dripping – Doctor Crippen
Drop – Lollipop
Drum – Finger and thumb
Drunk – Elephant's trunk

Ear – Glass of beer / King Lear / Southend Pier
Earner – Bunsen burner
Egg – Borrow and beg
Eye – Kidney pie
Eyes – Mince pies
Face – Boat race / Chevy Chase / Fillet of plaice / Glass case / Satin and lace
Faces – Airs and graces
Facts – Brass tacks / Tin tacks
Fag – Harry Wragg / Oily rag / Spit and drag
Fake – Corn flake / Sexton Blake
Fan – Isle of Man
Fart – Doyly Carte / Raspberry tart
Fat – Jack Sprat
Father – Soap and lather / Sorry and sad
Feet – Plates of meat
Fellow – Umbrella
Fence – Eighteen pence
Fever – Robinson and Cleaver
Fib – Spare rib
Fiddle – Hi Diddle Diddle
Fight – Left and right / Read and write
Fighter – Typewriter
File – Plymouth Argyll
Finger - Lean and linger
Fingernail – Slug and snail
Fire – Anna Maria / Black Maria / Jeremiah
Fish – Lillian Gish
Fist – Oliver Twist
Fiver – Deep sea diver / Lady Godiva / Sky diver
Fix – Seven and six
Flash – Pie and mash
Flat – This and that
Flea – Bonnie Dundee / You and me
Flies – Alderman's eyes
Flight – Read and write
Flowers – April showers / Early hours / Yours and ours
Fluke – Iron Duke
Flutter – Grumble and mutter
Fly – Meat pie
Flying Squad – Sweeney Todd
Folks – Soaks
Fool – Oats and barley / Muffin the Mule
Fork – Duke of York / Roast pork
Freemasonry lodge – Slither and dodge
Freeze – Stand at ease
Freezer – Julius Caesar
Friend – Mile End
Funnel – Blackwall Tunnel
Gaol – Bucket and pail / Ginger ale / Sorrowful tale
Garage – Horse and carriage
Garden – Beg your pardon / Dolly Varden
Geezer – Ice-cream freezer
Ghost – Pillar and post / Slice of toast

Gin – Brian O'Lynn / Needle and pin / Nell Gwyn / Thick and thin / Vera Lynn
Girl – Mother of Pearl / Ocean pearl / Pall Mall
Girls – Twists and twirls
Glove – Turtle dove
Glutton – Beef and mutton
Go – Scapa Flow
Good – Robin Hood / Wee Georgie Wood
Goods – Little Red Riding Hoods
Gout – Salmon and trout
Graft – George Raft
Grass – Ernie Marsh
Gravy – Army and Navy
Greek – Bubble and squeak
Greens – God save the Queens / Has beens / Nellie Deans
Grey – Night and day
Ground – Penny a pound / Safe and sound
Guards – Christmas cards
Guinness – Photo finish
Gun – Hot Cross Bun
Gut – Limehouse Cut
Guts – Newington Butts
Gutter – Bread and butter
Hag – Boiled rag
Hair – Barnet Fair / Lady Isobel
Ham – Trolley and tram
Handkerchief – Widow Twankey
Handle – Harry Randall
Hands – Elastic bands / German bands / Margate sands
Handy – Sugar candy
Hanky panky – Moody and Sankey
Harm – Chalk Farm
Hat – Ball of fat / This and that / Tit for tat
Head – Alive or dead / Crust of bread / Gingerbread / Loaf of bread / Toffee wrapper
Heart – Stop and start / Strawberry tart
Hell – Ding dong bell
Hide – Duck and dive
Hill – Jack and Jill
Hit – Fourpenny bit
Hole – Marry Old Soul
Home – Ham and bone / Pope of Rome
Horse – Bottle of sauce / Charing Cross / Smooth and coarse / Tomato sauce
Host – Dripping toast
Hot – Peas in the pot
House – Cat and mouse / Flea and louse / Micky Mouse / Rat and mouse
Husband – Telltytubby
Influenza – Inky blue
Informer – Grasshopper
Itch – Little Titch
Jacket – Steam packet
Japanese – Orange pip
Jeans – Baked beans / String beans

Jelly – Mother Kelly
Jew – Buckle me shoe / Four by two / Front wheel skid / God forbid / Half past two / Kangaroo / Quarter to two / Teapot lid
Jewellery – Tomfoolery
Joke – Gospel Oak
Joker – Tapioca
Judge – Barnaby Rudge / Inky smudge
Kettle – Hansel and Gretel / Scrap metal
Kid – Dustbin lid / Saucepan lid / Teapot lid
Kids – God forbids
Kip – Feather and flip
Kipper – Jack the Ripper
Kiss – Hit or miss
Kisses – Plates and dishes
Knackered – Christmas crackered
Knee – Trunk and tree
Knees – Biscuits and cheese / Bread and cheese
Knickers – Alan Whickers
Knife – Drum and fife / Man and wife
Kosher – Nova Scotia
Labour – Beggar-my-neighbour
Lace – Pig's face
Laces – Funny faces
Ladder – Blackadder
Ladies – Rosie O'Grady's
Lamb – Uncle Sam
Lamp – Sarah Gamp
Lark – Bushey Park
Late – Harry Tate / Tiddler's bait
Later – Alligator
Laugh – Cow and calf / Turkish bath
Lavatory – Rag and bone
Lawyer – Tom Sawyer

Lazy – Gert and Daisy
Lead – Crust of bread
Leg – Easter egg
Legs – Clothes pegs / Dutch pegs / Scotch eggs
Liar – Dunlop tyre / Holy friar / Town Crier
Lid – God forbid
Lie – Collar and tie
Lies – Pork pies
Life – Fork and knife / Struggle and strife
Light – Merry and bright / Widow's mite
Lights – Derby brights
Liver – Cheerful giver / Swanee River
Lodger – Artful Dodger / Jolly Roger
Look – Beecher's Brook / Butcher's hook / Thomas Cook
Looking glass – Snake in the grass
Loot – Forbidden fruit / Whistle and toot

Lorry – Annie Laurie / Safe and sorry
Lost – Jack Frost
Lousy – Housey-housey
Love – Heavens above / Turtle dove
Lunch – Judy and Punch
Mad – Mum and dad
Magistrate – Garden gate
Man – Pot and pan
Married – Cut and carried / Dot and carried
Marry – Cash and carry
Mat – Dog and cat
Match – Colney Hatch / Itch and scratch
Matches – Cuts and scratches
Mate – China plate
Meat – Dead beat
Melon – Mary Ellen
Mental – Radio Rental
Mess – Rudolph Hess
Mice – Apples and rice / Sacks of rice
Microphone – Yorkshire tyke
Milk – Charlie Dilke / Yellow silk
Minute – Cock linnet
Miss – Cuddle and kiss
Missus – Cheese and kisses / Hugs and kisses / Plates and dishes
Moke – Jerusalem artichoke
Money – Bees and honey / Bread and honey / Easter bunny / Pots of honey
Money – Sugar and honey
Moody – Punch and Judy
Morning – Day's a-dawning / Gypsy's warning
Mother – Finger and thumb / Love one another / One and t'other
Motor – Yarmouth bloater
Mouth – Deep South / North and south / Queen of the South
Muddle – Kiss and cuddle
Mug – Steam tug / Toby jug
Mugs – Hearth rugs
Murder – Iron girder
Nackered – Cream crackered
Nancy – Tickle your fancy
Nark – Noah's Ark
Natter – Henley Regatta
Navy – Pudding and gravy / Soup and gravy
Neck – Bushel and peck / Gregory Peck / Upper deck
Neighbour – Hard labour
Nerves – West Ham Reserves
Newspaper – Linen draper
Nice – Chicken and rice / Sugar and spice
Nick – Cow's lick / Moby Dick
Nightdress – God almighty
Nipper – Fly tipper
Noise – Box of toys / Girls and boys / Theydon Bois
Nose – Fireman's hose / I suppose / Irish Rose / Margaret Rose
Nutter – Bread and butter / Pound of butter
Odd – Tommy Dodd
Old – Silver and gold

Old woman – Gooseberry pudden
Onions – Corns and bunions
Order – Harry Lauder
Overcoat – Weasel and stoat
Paddock – Smoked haddock
Paddy – Goodie and baddie
Pads – Mums and dads
Pain – Park Lane / Petticoat Lane
Panel – English Channel / Soap and flannel
Pants – Fleas and ants / Soldier ants
Paper – Skyscraper
Pardon – Covent Garden
Park – Joan of Arc / Light and dark / Skylark
Parole – Jam roll
Party – Hale and hearty / Moriarty
Pawn – Bullock's horn
Pear – Teddy Bear
Peck – Tooting Bec
Penny – Abergavenny
Pension – Stand to attention
Pepper – High stepper
Pest – String vest / Woolly vest
Photograph – Kipper and bloater
Piano – Apple and banana / Joanna
Pickaxe – Paddy and Mick
Pickle – Slap and tickle
Pickles – Harvey Nichols
Pictures – Dolly mixtures
Piddle – Jimmy Riddle
Pie – Captain Bligh / Penny for the Guy
Piles – Chalfont St Giles / Farmer Giles / Laughs and smiles
Pill – Jack and Jill / Lord Hill
Pillow – Aston Villa / Max Miller / Tit willow / Weeping willow
Pillows – Rolling billows
Pinch – Half inch
Pink – Rinky-dink
Pint – Top joint
Pipe – Cherry ripe / Raw and ripe
Pissed – Brahms and Liszt / Hand and fist / Lloyd's List
Pissy – Aunt Cissie
Pitch – Hedge and ditch
Plain – Park Lane
Plate – Pearly Gate
Play – Night and day
Plug – Little Brown Jug
Pocket – Davy Crocket / Lucy Lockit / Skyrocket / Stephenson's Rocket
Police – Uncle Wilf
Pong – Hong Kong
Pony – Macaroni
Pools – April fools
Poor – On the floor
Pork – Duchess of York / Knife and fork
Porridge – Thyme and borage
Port – Casey's Court

Porter – Liffey Water
Poser – Carl Rosa
Post – Holy Ghost / Tea and toast
Pot of beer – Sir Walter Scott
Potato – Spanish waiter
Potatoes – Oscar Slaters / Rose buds
Pouffe – Collar and cuff
Pound – Lost and found / Merry go round / Plymouth Sound
Pox – Coachman on the box
Prat – Top hat
Price – Nits and lice / Snow and ice
Prick – Moby Dick
Priest – Bag of yeast
Prison – Hokey pokey
Prostitute - Brass nail / Early door / Jonah's whale / Six to four / Tug o'war
Prune – Rangoon
Public house – Battle cruiser / Rub-a-dub
Punter – Billy Bunter / Gazunder
Quaker – Muffin baker
Queer – Brighton Pier / Buccaneer / Ginger beer
Queue – Pot of glue
Quick – Lollipop stick
Quid – Saucepan lid
Race course – Iron horse
Races – Airs and graces / Belt and braces / Pair of braces
Rain – France and Spain / Pleasure and pain
Raining – Thistledown
Rat – Bowler hat / Top hat
Rates – Garden gates
Reader – Nose bleeder
Readies – Nelson Eddys
Refrigerator – Tower Bridge
Rent – Burton on Trent / Duke of Kent
Reporter – Sniffer and snorter
Rice – Three blind mice
Right – Harbour light / Isle of Wight
River – Shake and shiver
Road – Frog and toad
Roll – Toad in the hole
Room – Birch broom
Rotten – Needle and cotton / Reels of cotton
Round – Fox and hound
Row – Bull and cow
Rum – Finger and thumb / Kingdom come / Thimble and thumb / Tom Thumb
Run – Currant bun / Hot Cross Bun
Sack – Last card in the pack / Tin tack
Sad – Alan Ladd
Saw – Bear's paw / Mother-in-law
Scab – Hansom cab
Scar – Mars bar
Scarf – Arf and arf / Tin bath
Scats – Kilkenny cats
School – Pontypool

Scotch – Gold watch / Pimple and blotch
Scotland Yard – Bladder of lard
Screw – Little Boy Blue
Sea – Housemaid's knee
Sense – Eighteen pence / Shillings and pence
Shackle – Block and tackle
Shakes – Rattlesnakes
Share – Lion's lair / Vanity Fair
Shares – Rupert Bears
Shave - Chas and Dave / Dig in the grave / Ocean wave
Shed – King's Head
Shelter – Helter skelter
Sherry – Captain Merry / Londonderry / Woolwich Ferry
Shilling – Door knob / One for his nob / Rogue and villain / Thomas Tilling
Shiner – Morris Minor
Ship – 'A'penny dip
Shirt – Dicky Dirt / Uncle Bert
Shirty – Uncle Bertie
Shit – Tom Tit
Shits – Two bob bits
Shoe – Canoe / Red, white, and blue
Shoes – Ps and qs
Shoot – Put in the boot
Shop – Lollipop
Shoulder – Cigarette holder
Shoulders – Rocks and boulders
Shovel – Lord Lovell
Shower – Eiffel Tower
Sick – Moby Dick / Spotted Dick / Tom and Dick / Uncle Dick
Silk – Cat's milk
Silly – Daffadown Dilly / Piccadilly / Uncle Willie
Sing – Highland fling
Sing song – Ding dong
Singer – Mangle and wringer
Sister – Skin and blister
Skint – Boracic lint
Skive – Duck and dive
Skiver – Screwdriver
Sky – Apple pie / Shepherd's pie
Slash – Johnny Cash
Sleep - Bo Peep
Slipper – Jack the Ripper
Slippers – Pair of kippers / Yankee clippers
Smack – Uncle Mac
Smasher – Gammon rasher
Smell – Heaven and hell / William Tell
Smile – Penny a mile / River Nile
Smoke – Cough and choke / Laugh and joke / Old oak
Smokes – Ash and oaks
Sneeze – Bread and cheese
Snide – Jekyll and Hyde
Snitch – Half hitch
Snore – Lions roar
Snout – Salmon and trout

Snow – Buck and doe / To and fro
Soap – Band of Hope / Cape of Good Hope
Socks – Almond rocks / Grimsby Docks / Katherine Docks / Tilbury Docks
Son – Bath bun / Chelsea bun / Hot Cross Bun / Sticky bun
Sot – Pint pot
Soup – Loop the loop
Sovereign – Jimmy O'Goblin
Sparks – Groucho Marx
Sparrow - Bow and arrow
Spats – Wanstead Flats
Spectacles – Hackney Marshes / Lancashire lasses / Mountain passes / Working classes
Spider – Apple cider / Sit beside her
Spoon – Blue moon / Lorna Doone
Spruce – Madam de Luce
Spunk – Maria Monk
Squadron Leader – Squabbling bleeder
Squatter – Pig's trotter
Stage – Greengage / Handley Page
Stairs – Apples and pears / Troubles and cares
Stake – Joe Blake
Stalls – Niagara Falls
Star – La-Di-Da
Starch – Marble Arch
Start – Puff and dart
State – Harry Tate / Six and eight / Two and eight
Stays – Bryant and Mays
Steak – Quiver and shake / Sexton Blake
Stew – How D'ye Do / Waterloo
Stick – Paddy Quick
Stink – Pen and ink
Stir – Ben Hur / Joe Gurr
Stocking – Reeling and rocking
Stools – April fools
Stout – In and Out
Straight – Six and eight
Strange – Home on the range
Strangers – Glasgow Rangers / Queen's Park Rangers
Street – Field of wheat / Plates of meat
Stretch – Jack Ketch
Stripper – Herring and kipper
Style – Tate and Lyle
Suit – Whistle and flute
Sun – Bath bun
Supper – Tommy Tucker
Survive – Duck and dive
Swear – Lord Mayor / Rip and tear
Sweetheart – Jam tart
Table – Cain and Able
Tailor – Maidstone jailer / Sinbad the Sailor
Tale – Hill and dale / Weep and wail
Talk – Duke of York / Rabbit and pork
Tanner – Bicycle spanner / Lord of the Manor / Tartan banner
Tap – Cellar flap

Tea – Jenny Lee / Nancy Lea / River Lea / Rosie Lee / You and me
Teeth – Edward Heath / Hampstead Heath / Hounslow Heath / Roast beef
Telephone – Dog and bone / Eau de Cologne / Mary Malone / Molly Malone / Trombone
Television – Custard and jelly / Marie Corelli / Mother Kelly
Ten pound note – Ayrton Senna / Cock and hen
Ten shillings – Shower bath
Thick – Paddy and Mick / Paddy Quick
Thief – Tea leaf
Thighs – Nelly Bly's / Songs and sighs
Thin – Needle and pin
Throat – Hairy goat / Nanny goat
Thumb – Jamaica rum
Thunder – Up and under
Ticket – Bat and wicket
Tie – Fourth of July / Mud in your eye / Peckham Rye
Tight – Isle of Wight / Turkish delight
Tights – Fly by nights / Snow Whites
Till – Benny Hill / Jack and Jill
Time – Bird lime / Lemon and lime
Toast – Holy Ghost / Pig and roast
Tobacco – Hi Jimmy Knacker
Toe – Stop and go
Toes – These and those
Tongue - Brewer's bung
Tools – April fools
Tooth – General Booth
Torch – Back porch
Tote – Canal boat / Nanny goat
Tout – Brussels sprout
Town – Joe Brown
Traffic warden – Gay Gordon
Train – Hail and rain / John Wayne / Struggle and strain
Trainers – Strugglers and strainers
Tram – Baa-lamb / Bread and jam / Plate of ham
Tramp – Halfpenny stamp / Hurricane lamp
Tray – Vicar of Bray
Trick – Lollipop stick
Trip over – Come a clover
Tripe – Cherry ripe
Trouble – Barney Rubble

Trousers – Council houses / Dan Dares / Round the houses / Rowton Houses

True – Eyes of blue / Irish stew
Tube – Oxo cube
Tune – Stewed prune
Turd – Richard the Third
Twig – Earwig
Umbrella – Aunt Ella / Cousin Ella / Stan and Ollie
Undertaker – Overcoat maker
Urinate – Gypsy's kiss / Hit and miss Riddle-me-ree / Rip Van Winkle / Southend on Sea
Van – Peter Pan
Vest – East and west / Sunday best
Villain – Bernard Dillon
Voice – Hobson's choice / Rolls Royce
Wages – Greengages / Rock of Ages
Waistcoat – Charley Prescott / Jim Prescott
Waiter – Baked potato / Cheese grater / Cold potato / Hot potato
Walk – Ball of chalk
Walks – Guy Fawkes
Wash – Bob Squash
Watch – Gordon and Gotch
Water – Fireman's daughter / Mother and daughter / Neptune's daughter
Weak – Bubble and squeak
Weather – Hat and feather / Tar and feather
Week – Bubble and squeak
Welshmen – Riff-raff
West – Jacket and vest
Whiskers – Brothers and sisters
Whisky – Bright and frisky / Gay and frisky
Wife – Carving knife / Drum and fife / Duchess of Fife / Fork and knife / Sporting Life / Storm and strife / Struggle and strife
Wife – Trouble and strife
Wig – Guinea pig / Irish jig / Syrup of figs
Win – Nose and chin
Wind – Jenny Lind
Window – Burnt cinder / Polly Flinder / Tommy Trinder
Windy – Rawalpindi
Wine – Rise and shine
Wishes – Pots and dishes
Word – Dicky bird / Early bird

Work – Dunkirk / Terrible Turk
World – Flag unfurled
Wrong – Hong Kong
Yank – Ham shank
Yanks – Army tanks

BIBLIOGRAPHY

Brewer's Dictionary of phrase and fable
Casebook of Sherlock Doyle, by Harry Stone, 1991
Chambers Dictionary of world history, 1993
Concise Dictionary of National Biography, OUP
Dictionary of dates, Dent, 1942
Handbook to the environs of London, by James Thorne, 1876
Highways and byways in London, by Mrs F T Cook, 1902
History of British bus services, by John Hibbs, 1968
The last actor-managers, by Hesketh Pearson, 1950
A load of Cockney cobblers, by Bob Aylwin, 1973
Oxford Companion to English literature
Oxford Dictionary of phrase and fable
Oxford Dictionary of Quotations
Penguin Dictionary of Quotations
Reader's Digest Universal Dictionary
Twentieth century crime and mystery writers, Macmillan
Songs of the British music hall, by Peter Davison
1000 makers of the twentieth century, edited Godfrey Smith, 1971

Other etymological dictionaries available in this series –

Dijja wanna say sumpfing? A guide to Estuary English
The speech used by Darren and Tracy who live between London and Saffend, together with a clutch of recipes for South Essex man

Newspeak: A dictionary of modern English phraseology
When politicians, Council officials and superior journalists wish to confuse and obfuscate they lapse into this jargon that needs a dictionary to translate it – this is it!